T0319098

Cambridge Elements ☰

Elements in Campaigns and Elections
edited by
R. Michael Alvarez
California Institute of Technology
Emily Beaulieu Bacchus
University of Kentucky
Charles Stewart III
Massachusetts Institute of Technology

THE REPRESENTATIONAL CONSEQUENCES OF ELECTRONIC VOTING REFORM

Evidence from Argentina

Santiago Alles
Universidad de San Andrés

Tiffany D. Barnes
University of Kentucky

Carolina Tchintian
CIPPEC-UBA-UTDT

CAMBRIDGE
UNIVERSITY PRESS

Shaftesbury Road, Cambridge CB2 8EA, United Kingdom

One Liberty Plaza, 20th Floor, New York, NY 10006, USA

477 Williamstown Road, Port Melbourne, VIC 3207, Australia

314–321, 3rd Floor, Plot 3, Splendor Forum, Jasola District Centre,
New Delhi – 110025, India

103 Penang Road, #05–06/07, Visioncrest Commercial, Singapore 238467

Cambridge University Press is part of Cambridge University Press & Assessment,
a department of the University of Cambridge.

We share the University's mission to contribute to society through the pursuit of
education, learning and research at the highest international levels of excellence.

www.cambridge.org
Information on this title: www.cambridge.org/9781108978293

DOI: 10.1017/9781108973960

© Santiago Alles, Tiffany D. Barnes, and Carolina Tchintian 2023

This publication is in copyright. Subject to statutory exception and to the provisions
of relevant collective licensing agreements, no reproduction of any part may take
place without the written permission of Cambridge University Press & Assessment.

First published 2023

A catalogue record for this publication is available from the British Library.

ISBN 978-1-108-97829-3 Paperback
ISSN 2633-0970 (online)
ISSN 2633-0962 (print)

Additional resources for this publication at Cambridge.org/Alles.

Cambridge University Press & Assessment has no responsibility for the persistence
or accuracy of URLs for external or third-party internet websites referred to in this
publication and does not guarantee that any content on such websites is, or will
remain, accurate or appropriate.

The Representational Consequences of Electronic Voting Reform

Evidence from Argentina

Elements in Campaigns and Elections

DOI: 10.1017/9781108973960
First published online: May 2023

Santiago Alles
Universidad de San Andrés

Tiffany D. Barnes
University of Kentucky

Carolina Tchintian
CIPPEC-UBA-UTDT

Author for correspondence: Santiago Alles, salles@udesa.edu.ar

Abstract: Ballots and voting devices are fundamental tools in the electoral process. Despite their importance, scholars have paid little attention to the broader implications of voting procedures. The authors contend that ballots have significant implications for democratic representation, as they affect the cost associated with voting for citizens and electioneering for elites. This Element explains how ballot designs affect the behavior of voters, the performance of candidates, and the strategies of parties. The Element shows how voting procedures structure the likelihood of vote splitting and ballot roll-off. This in turn has implications for candidates. Focusing on gender and experience, the Element also shows how ballot form alters the salience of personal vote-earning attributes. With respect to political parties, ballot structure can shift the cost, strategies, and ultimately electoral fortunes of political parties. Finally, the Element discusses the profound implications ballot forms have for party campaigns and election outcomes.

Keywords: ballot design, voting procedures, electoral institutions, political institutions, Latin American politics

© Santiago Alles, Tiffany D. Barnes, and Carolina Tchintian 2023

ISBNs: 9781108978293 (PB), 9781108973960 (OC)
ISSNs: 2633-0970 (online), 2633-0962 (print)

Contents

Further online supplementary material (online appendix)
can be accessed at Cambridge.org/Alles

1 Introduction

Democracy rests on the idea that the government should reflect the will of the people. In practice, however, democratic institutions vary dramatically in their representativeness. Whereas some institutions are designed to represent a diversity of interests, forcing parties to share power, other institutions manufacture majorities, prioritizing effective government over representation. As a result of institutional design, groups face varying levels of access and inclusion. Copious research seeks to understand the trade-offs in electoral institutions and how different electoral rules and procedures can increase the representation of different groups in society, ranging from small political parties to women and ethnic minorities.

Ballots and voting devices, in particular, are fundamental tools in the electoral process (Barnes et al. 2017; Calvo et al. 2009; Engstrom and Roberts 2020; Katz et al. 2011). The voting instrument connects competing candidates and parties with voters. Notably, there is substantial variation in the design of ballots and voting devices used around the democratic world (Herrnson et al. 2008; Reynolds and Steenbergen 2006). Ballots differ in how candidates and parties are displayed, either organized along party or office lines. Ballots differ in how voters must indicate their choices, for example marking a box, punching a card, or manually tearing the ballot. Ballots differ in the use of photographs of candidates and party logos. Ballots involve different transmission devices, ranging from paper alone to electronic machines. Even in cases when all other electoral rules remain the same, voting procedures vary across countries, within countries, and over time.

Despite the importance of ballots and associated voting procedures, scholars have paid little attention to the ways that these features of elections shape representation. Although many scholars have investigated the adoption of electronic voting, most have done so with an eye toward electoral integrity (e.g., Alvarez et al. 2018; Beaulieu 2014, 2016). In this Element, we argue that there can be important representational consequences associated with the adoption of electronic voting and the way the electoral offer is presented on the ballot. We contend that any changes to the ballot may have significant implications for democratic representation, as they affect the cost of voting for citizens and electioneering for elites. The precise consequences of a reform will, of course, depend on the procedure that was previously in place and the way the new voting instrument interacts with the other electoral rules in place. In this Element, we leverage an electronic voting reform that resulted in modifications to the existing ballot to demonstrate how ballot designs affect the behavior of voters, the performance of candidates, and the strategies of parties.

Ballot Design and Representational Consequences: Voters,
Candidates, and Parties

Ballot designs have important consequences for what happens in the voting booth (Barnes et al. 2017; Engstrom and Roberts 2020; Muraoka 2021; Rusk 1970; Tchintian 2018). In this Element, we take the voting booth as a starting point, assessing the consequences of ballot design on voter's behavior at the polls. Then, we consider the representational ramifications of these behavioral changes, looking into the broader implications of ballot design for the entire electoral process.

In thinking about voters, voting demands time and effort. The manner in which the electoral offer is presented to voters, and the process through which votes are cast, influence how voters' preferences are translated into outcomes. More complicated processes may discourage some citizens from fully expressing their preferences at the polls. Consider, for instance, the case of partisan paper ballots – a ballot that requires voters to physically tear a piece of paper in order to split their vote. For a voter who prefers to vote for candidates from different parties in different contests at stake (i.e., split-ticket voting), this ballot is more demanding than the one that simply requires voters to check a box associated with each candidate in each race. Whereas the former is likely to encourage straight-ticket voting, the latter is likely to facilitate split-ticket voting.

The same ballot that encourages split-ticket voting also discourages roll-off (i.e., when voters cast a valid vote for candidates at the top of the ballot but not for candidates further down the ballot). For example, some ballot structures automatically reengage voters in the voting process each time they split their ballot by presenting them with the slate of candidates for subsequent contests on successive screens. This structure makes it easy for voters to vote in subsequent contests, even if they choose to split their ballot. This is because the ballot requires voters to actively choose an option, either to vote for a candidate or to vote blank, rather than simply allowing them to discard the bottom portion of the ballot after tearing the ballot in two. Ballots that require, or even encourage, voters to make a decision for every contest at stake decrease roll-off.

Voters' behavior subsequently informs parties' and candidates' strategic electioneering decisions. With respect to candidates, a ballot form that facilitates split-ticket voting undermines the strength of the coattails at the top of the ticket. Since voters are more likely to make separate choices for each contest at stake, personal vote-earning attributes or other information cues may be more salient for down-ballot candidates than in contexts that facilitate straight-ticket voting. The added emphasis on personal vote-earning attributes in down-ballot races may ultimately strengthen candidates' incentives to cultivate a personal reputation.

As for parties, when voters make discrete choices for each race, the opportunities to center campaigns around specific races grow substantially. Small parties that are not viable in executive races (e.g., presidential or gubernatorial) may focus their efforts on campaigning for their legislative candidates. When electoral rules require individual political parties to procure and distribute their own ballots to polling stations, parties are incentivized to concentrate their campaign resources in geographical areas where they will get a larger electoral payoff. Smaller parties may forgo distributing ballots across the entire district – as doing so is costly – and concentrate exclusively on areas where they can count on local networks to fill in logistic campaign roles. But, if the election authority is responsible for printing and distributing ballots across the entire territory, smaller political parties will face lower constraints when planning where to campaign. Consequently, we expect to observe a more homogeneous geographical distribution of votes when the electoral authority guarantees the provision of ballots at every voting booth than under electoral rules where parties are responsible for filling that role.

Exploiting an Incremental Ballot Reform: A Quasi-Experiment

To investigate the representational consequences of ballot design, this Element takes advantage of a ballot reform in Argentina, in which electronic voting was incrementally implemented. We exploit observational data from seven consecutive election cycles, over a twelve-year period, when a province in Argentina switched from partisan paper ballots to electronically administered Australian ballots.[1] In Section 2, we describe the procedures for voting using the partisan paper ballots compared to the electronically administered ballot, and we explain how the ballot reform was implemented across the province. To examine the ballot effects on voters, candidates, and parties, we develop two main identification strategies in the subsequent sections.

First, in Section 3, we test our expectations about voters. We employ a quasi-experimental design, leveraging the simultaneous use of the two voting procedures – the traditional partisan paper ballots in some precincts compared to the electronically administered Australian ballots in other precincts – to examine how the ballot form affects individual choices, such as split-ticket voting and ballot roll-off. We use matching techniques to address threats to random

---

[1] We use the terms partisan paper ballots, paper ballots, and the ballot-and-envelope system interchangeably. When referencing this ballot reform in Argentina, we use the terms electronic ballot and electronic devices interchangeably. A detailed description of the adopted procedure is provided in: Tribunal Electoral de la Provincia de Salta. 2019. "Manual de Capacitación para Autoridades de Mesa. Sistema de Boleta Única Electrónica." www.electoralsalta.gob.ar/informa cion/2019/manual-de-capacitacion-2019.pdf (accessed October 15, 2022).

assignment and a difference-in-difference (DiD) approach to estimate the ballot effect. This same strategy is used to test the ballot effect on electoral coordination in Section 6 and is used to provide supplementary evidence in Section 4 regarding the ballot effect on incumbency advantage.

Second, we employ cross-sectional statistical analyses to examine how the ballot form affects the performance of candidates and the strategies of parties. In Section 4, we examine municipality-level data from about 1,200 mayoral candidates between 2007 and 2019 to assess the effects of the ballot form on the performance of incumbent and women candidates. Finally, turning to the ballot implications for parties, in Section 5 we rely on department-level data from about 950 province House and Senate party lists between 2009 and 2019.

The Importance of Studying Ballot Structure

This Element contributes to a growing body of research investigating the effects of ballot forms and voting procedures on elections and representation. Ballots differ in terms of the cognitive and physical demands they place on voters, ultimately affecting their behavior. Critical features range from the length of the ballot (Aguilar et al. 2015; Darcy and Schneider 1989; Walker 1966; Wattenberg et al. 2000) and the order and placement of parties and candidates (Casas et al. 2020; Ho and Imai 2008; Miller and Krosnick 1998; Söderlund et al. 2021; Ortega Villodres 2008) to the inclusion of informational cues such as pictures, images, and party symbols (Banducci et al. 2008; Kimball and Kropf 2005; Moehler and Conroy-Krutz 2016; Tchintian 2018).

One of the most well-trodden ballot design questions addressed by political science is whether the ballot form affects how voters translate their preferences into votes. Though voters may prefer to split the ticket for a variety of reasons, such as producing partisan balance (Burden and Helmke 2009) or voting strategically to avoid wasting their vote (Cox 1997; Moser and Scheiner 2009), the decision to split the ballot is conditioned by ballot design (Barnes et al. 2017; Darcy and Schneider 1989; Tchintian 2018; Walker 1966).

Complicated ballots may also result in the omission of voter's preferences. In the case of Japan, for instance, voters are required to write candidates' names on a blank ballot. Muraoka (2021) demonstrates that voters may forgo voting for their most preferred candidate when the candidate's name is sufficiently complex, and instead opt for an easier name to write. Similarly, some ballot structures may cause confusion and frustration for voters, ultimately increasing the number of mistaken, invalid, and/or unrecorded votes (Ansolabehere and Stewart 2005; Hanmer et al. 2010; Kimball and Kropf 2005; Pachón et al. 2017; Sievert 2020).

Importantly, such errors might not be randomly distributed. Instead, they may be biased against particular groups of voters such as ethnic minorities and the less educated (Engstrom and Roberts 2020; Tomz and Van Houweling 2003). Complicated ballots may even deter voters from turning out when voting is not mandatory, as is the case with the elimination of straight-ticket voting in the United States (Engstrom 2012).

Candidates and Parties

Scholars have considered how ballot designs and election administration shape what happens in the voting booth (e.g., split-ticket voting, roll-off, unintentional under/over vote), but far less research attempts to understand how ballot features affect behavior beyond the polls. A primary contribution of this Element is to move beyond the voting booth. In doing so, we build on recent studies that advance our considerations of how ballot types shape representational outcomes more broadly. To understand this contribution, it is important to briefly review what we know about the relationship between ballot features and candidates' and parties' behavior.

With respect to candidates, ballots affect the extent and importance of either cultivating the personal vote or relying on the relevance of the party machinery to advance one's electoral fortunes (Engstrom and Roberts 2020). Ballot structures can also strengthen (or weaken) the electoral connection and legislative responsiveness of representatives once in office (Katz and Sala 1996; Wittrock et al. 2008). Engstrom and Roberts (2020) consider how the ballot type shapes legislative behavior, by affecting which candidates succeed at the polls. They argue that ballots that are organized by the office at stake, rather than by political party, heighten the importance of candidates' name recognition. Name recognition is so much stronger for candidates competing under office-centered ballots that they "scare off" challengers. This, in turn, has a host of implications for how legislators behave once in office. Engstrom and Roberts demonstrate that US Members of Congress who depend more on name recognition to get into office spend more time cultivating their own personal reputation – sponsoring more legislation, exercising more discretion when siding with the president, and being more effective legislators.

Tchintian (2018) similarly shows how ballot design alters the significance of personal attributes in elections. Using survey and observational data from El Salvador and Ecuador, she examines whether candidates' personal attributes in their ballot pictures affect the probability of being elected. She finds that personal attributes are important, but the weight of these factors varies depending on ballot design features. The fate of candidates featured on longer or crowded ballots is closely tied to the attributes conveyed by their ballot image, especially for candidates who are at the bottom of the ticket. In another study, taking advantage of a ballot reform in Brazil, Tchintian shows that when legislators' pictures are featured on the ballots, candidates respond by breaking with party ranks more frequently – voting independent of their party in an effort to make a name for themselves. We extend this logic to consider how other personal vote-earning attributes, in our case gender, shape candidates' success at the polls.

From the parties' perspective, voting procedures vary in terms of the effort demanded by elites to maximize their electoral results, and thus parties' campaign strategies and performance (Alles et al. 2021). Although scholars have paid less attention to the implication of ballot reform on parties' behavior, there are some notable exceptions (Alles et al. 2021; Engstrom and Roberts 2020; Heckelman 2000).

In Colombia, for instance, partisan paper ballots were replaced by Australian ballots in the early 1990s. Whereas prior to the Australian ballot not every candidate or every party was able to coordinate and finance the distribution of their ballot, the adoption of the Australian ballot guaranteed that every party and every candidate was present at the ballot box everywhere, regardless of their campaign resources. Parties, and most especially the smaller ones, took advantage of the newfound universal distribution of ballots by extending the geographical coverage of their campaigns, appealing to new electoral audiences, and reshaping their bases. Moreover, the transformation of campaigning strategies undermined the territorial machines of traditional parties. Local leaders, who used to control well-organized mobilization networks, now faced the rise of new competitors in their electoral strongholds (Alles et al. 2021).

The adoption of the secret ballot in the United States likewise changed parties' strategies. As party bosses could no longer verify how constituents voted with the advent of the secret ballot, they were dissuaded from buying and selling votes – ultimately forcing parties to rely on different strategies to cultivate voters' support (Heckelman 2000). Some ballot features also make it harder to turn out voters. In the United States, the abolition of straight-ticket voting in some state elections made voting more costly for voters who preferred to vote straight-ticket (Engstrom and Roberts 2020). Absent a straight-ticket voting option, it takes individual voters more time to fill out their ballot, and the extra time individuals spend at the ballot box accumulates in longer lines at the polls, discouraging voters from turning out. Engstrom and Roberts find that African-American neighborhoods were more likely to be inflicted with longer lines and subsequently lower turnout. Given that African-Americans are a key stronghold of the Democratic Party, the suppression of African-American voters, no doubt, has implications for how the Democratic Party mobilizes and campaigns to this key constituency.

Ballot Design in Comparative Perspective

Ballot structures vary dramatically across and within countries, and yet comparative politics scholars have rarely considered how ballot types influence the way voters translate their preferences into votes and how elites react with different strategies. There are, of course, notable exceptions. As mentioned as previously noted, Tchintian (2018) considers a number of cases across Latin America, including El Salvador and Honduras. Alles, Pachón, and Muñoz (2021) likewise provide an extensive treatment to the ballot reform in Colombia. Muraoka (2021) illustrates the unintended implications of ballot design in Japan.

Electronic voting reform has received considerable attention cross-nationally. Many countries have adopted electronic voting over the last twenty years in an attempt to improve electoral processes by offering more user-friendly procedures for voters, bolstering confidence in elections, and automating vote tallying (Alvarez and Hall 2008; Alvarez et al. 2009; 2011; Beaulieu 2014, 2016; Tchintian 2018; Tula 2005). The adoption of electronic voting in Salta, Argentina, along with a handful of reforms in other provinces throughout Argentina, has gained notable attention (Barnes et al. 2017; Dodyk and Nicolini 2017; Pomares et al. 2014).

Though scholars have started thinking about the broader representational consequences of voting procedures and extending this work beyond the United States (Alles et al. 2021; Barnes, Tchintian and Alles 2017; Calvo et al. 2009; Katz et al. 2011), more attention is needed to understand the ways that seemingly small adjustments to the ballot affect the entire political process (Engstrom and Roberts 2020). This Element extends this research, offering one of the first comprehensive studies of the consequences of ballot structure for voters, candidates, and parties beyond the United States.

The Critical Impact of the Ballot

The findings in this Element indicate that the ballot structure influences voters, candidates, and parties. With respect to voters, the change from partisan paper ballots to an electronically administered Australian ballot has significantly increased the share of split-ticket voting, resulting in a composition of the legislative assembly that is more independent from the results of the executive race. At the same time, the electronic devices are linked to a substantial reduction of ballot roll-off. A larger number of voters engaged in down-ballot races as compared to elections using the paper ballots, invigorating the democratic legitimacy of elected local officials.

As for candidates, electronic devices have heterogeneous effects on candidates competing in down-ballot races. Whereas the ballot form exerts only a weak influence over the electoral fates of women (compared to men) mayoral candidates, incumbent candidates enjoy a significant bonus in elections using electronic devices. Incumbent mayors standing for reelection, already natural front-runners, are uniquely positioned to exploit the increased salience of the personal vote afforded by the electronic Australian ballot.

Finally, as for political parties, we focus on two phenomena. First, different ballot forms involve different logistical burdens that affect the strategic response of parties. When parties are responsible for the provision of ballots to each voting center, some small parties without the resources to distribute ballots to all voting centers choose to concentrate their efforts in a limited area. This results in a geographically concentrated distribution of votes for their party. Under the electronically administered Australian ballot, parties are no longer responsible for the provision of ballots. Instead, it guarantees that all party options are available in every voting booth. For this reason, small political parties with fewer resources can expand the geographical reach of their campaign, resulting in a more homogeneous geographical distribution of votes.

Second, our findings show that parties adapt their campaign strategies to take advantage of the opportunities created by the ballot structure. Because the electronic devices eased vote splitting, the legislative election became more independent from the gubernatorial race. Some parties (though not all) were able to exploit this environment, encouraging voters to split their ballots, and attract a significant portion of new disposable votes to the legislative portion of their ticket. This facilitates the election of small parties to the legislature.

The remainder of the Element is organized as follows. Section 2 introduces the ballot reform. Section 3 examines how electronic voting reform influences voters' behavior. Then, Section 4 turns to the implications of reform for individual candidates. Sections 5 and 6 analyze the influence of electronic voting reform on political parties. The final section concludes, discussing the implications of this Element for electoral institutions and reform.

2 Electronic Voting in Salta: From Adoption to Implementation

Voting instruments have changed significantly over time. In Latin America, the first era of ballot reforms was centered on the adoption of the secret ballot (Hartlyn and Valenzuela 1995). Argentina and Uruguay established secret balloting in the 1910s, followed by Chile and Costa Rica a few years later.

Despite periodic elections, with few exceptions, democratic institutions did not consolidate until the 1980s, when a wave of democratization swept throughout the entire region (Hagopian and Mainwaring 2005). In this context of democratic transitions, a more careful design of electoral institutions came to be seen as a tool to foster stable democracies. Recent decades have witnessed reforms in voting procedures in numerous countries around the world seeking to make elections more efficient and reliable. In this respect, Latin American democracies have presented an active laboratory of innovation (Reynolds and Steenbergen 2006).

Historically, two types of ballot forms were widely used in the region. A first ballot type is the partisan paper ballot – also common in the United States in the nineteenth century (Engstrom and Kernell 2014). As Reynolds and Steenbergen (2006: 573) describe it, a partisan paper ballot is "a system where voters deposit a pre-printed party or candidate ballot in the ballot box – usually no mark is made on the pre-printed ballot. Oftentimes this system is accompanied by the use of envelopes for the ballots placed in the box." Often the electoral authority delegates the responsibility for printing and distributing the ballots to parties and candidates. This form has some comparative advantages in terms of implementation, namely, it is not technologically demanding for election administrators, and it is not cognitively demanding for voters. Still, these advantages come with clear trade-offs. Critics voiced concerns about inefficiencies, the burdens partisan paper ballots impose on political parties, and the opportunities it creates for election corruption, such as ballot theft and ballot sabotage.

A second ballot type, the Australian ballot, is a procedure in which voters use a uniform ballot that presents all the parties and candidates on a single ticket. Voters express their preference with a mark on the ballot, before depositing it in the ballot box. The Australian ballot refers to a family of ballot forms that include a variety of designs. The most important distinction within this group is whether they are arranged on party or office lines. A ballot organized on party line highlights candidates' attachment to parties, providing a clear partisan clue to voters. Ballots arranged on office line water down party linkages, forcing voters to make a deliberate effort when they want to vote for the same party across races.

As criticisms of the partisan paper ballot gained more traction over time, and as countries sought to modernize their electoral administration, the partisan paper ballots were gradually replaced by Australian ballots. Chile, for example, adopted an Australian ballot in 1958, long before the last wave of democratization, seeking to prevent voting corruption (Gamboa 2011). Similarly, Colombia abandoned partisan paper ballots in favor of an Australian ballot in 1991, and it has been used in every election since then, both electing national and local

Figure 1 Voting procedures in Latin America

Note: The figure presents the ballot form used in national elections by Latin American countries in the most recent election cycle prior to 2021.

offices (Alles et al. 2021; Pachón and Shugart 2010). The landscape in the region is currently dominated by the use of some form of Australian paper ballot in national elections, as shown in Figure 1, listing the ballot form used in the most recent election cycle. By 2021, only Argentina and Uruguay continued employing partisan ballots in national elections.

The adoption of electronic voting, although limited worldwide, has been part of this wave of reforms. Brazil features the largest implementation of electronic voting in the region. Between the late 1990s and early 2000s, Brazil gradually replaced paper ballots with electronic devices. Today electronic ballots are used for the election of all elected officials across every level of government in Brazil (Nicolau 2012). The reform has often been praised as successful in enfranchising voters of lower socioeconomic status (Fujiwara 2015) and in reducing blank and spoiled ballots (Nicolau 2015).

Other countries have adopted or piloted electronic devices. Venezuela implemented electronic voting in 1998. Notwithstanding a few minor changes, the procedure was still in place more than 20 years later. The use of electronic voting in Paraguay, by contrast, was short-lived. It was implemented at the national level in 2001, but its use was discontinued in 2007. Electronic voting has been piloted or adopted in a limited number of local elections in Argentina, Perú, Ecuador, Guatemala, and México (Alvarez et al. 2009; Di Primio 2019).

Since 2003, numerous provinces across Argentina have undertaken voting reforms. The election of subnational offices is regulated by provincial constitutions and laws (Calvo and Escolar 2005; Calvo and Micozzi 2005), and each province has its own electoral authorities in charge of conducting province-level

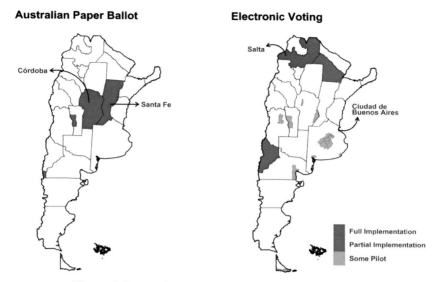

Figure 2 Innovations in voting procedures in Argentina

Note: The figure presents the ballot innovations piloted or adopted in subnational elections in Argentina between 2003 and 2021: Santa Fe and Córdoba adopted paper-based Australian ballots in 2011, while Salta and the City of Buenos Aires fully implemented electronic voting at least once

Source: Tile map by INDEC <www.indec.gob.ar/indec/web/Institucional-Indec-Codgeo>

elections. Although electoral rules vary considerably across provinces, until recently, all the provinces used the same partisan paper ballot. Figure 2 illustrates the scope of the ballot innovations across Argentina.[2] Two provinces, Santa Fe and Córdoba, adopted paper-based Australian ballots in 2011 for all provincial and local elections. Despite the dominance of the Australian ballot across Latin America, just a few municipalities in other provinces have emulated Santa Fe and Córdoba, and only did so partially.

Electronic voting has attracted relatively more attention from Argentine reformers. Thirteen provinces currently allow the use of some type of electronic device in province and local elections (Observatorio Político Electoral 2021), but the scope of the implementation has varied widely. The province of Salta and the City of Buenos Aires have used electronic voting across the entire district to elect the executive and the assembly in at least one election, though Buenos Aires subsequently discontinued its use. Two other provinces, Neuquén and Chaco, began gradual but incomplete adoption throughout their districts. Of all the cases of electronic voting adoption in Argentina, Salta was the first and most resolute implementer.

---

[2] For an extended discussion of variation in voting procedures across subnational elections in Argentina, see Appendix I.

From Partisan Paper Ballots to Electronic Voting: The Case of Salta, Argentina

This Element examines the ballot reform in Salta to understand the representational consequences of electronic voting reform. Over the course of several years, Salta implemented electronic voting in province and local elections. To understand the representational consequences of this ballot reform, it is necessary to be familiar with the original ballot structure in place and with the changes to the ballot introduced by electronic voting. Here, we detail the traditional partisan paper ballot that has historically been used throughout Argentina. Then, we discuss the adoption of the electronic Australian ballot across Salta.

The Partisan Paper Ballot

Before the midterm election in 2009, every precinct in Salta used partisan paper ballots that were ubiquitous across Argentina. In this system every political party has its own ballot. That is, only one political party is featured on each ballot. The ballot, as it is depicted in Figure 3 (pictures A to C), contained all of the party's candidates for each contest at stake. Each election at stake is displayed side-by-side, on a single piece of paper, and divided by a dashed line. This ballot design has several important consequences for political parties, candidates, and voters alike.

First, and perhaps most obviously, the ballot design has implications for voters. To cast a vote, the voter enters a private voting booth where she finds the ballots of all contending political parties displayed on a table, organized by party or coalition ID number in ascending order. Ballots contain the name, number, and logo of the party, the name of the candidates, and sometimes pictures of the candidates at the top of the ticket.

To cast a straight ticket vote, the voter simply chooses the party's ballot of her preference, folds it up, places it into the envelope, and slips the envelope into the ballot box. But, when the voter chooses to split her vote, the process is more demanding. To cast a split-ticket vote, the voter must physically "split" the ballot by cutting out the elected position she supports from each party. Then, she must put the pieces of the ballot that correspond to the candidates she supports in the envelope and deposit the envelope into the ballot box.

For instance, a voter chooses to vote Party A's candidate for governor and Party B's candidate for the provincial assembly. To do this, she must cut out the gubernatorial portion of the Party A ballot and place it in the envelope. Then, she must cut out the portion of the Party B ballot with the legislative candidates

Partisan Paper Ballots

Figure 3 Examples of paper and electronic ballots in Argentina

Note: The first three pictures present examples of partisan paper ballots, two from provincial elections in Salta (pictures A and B), and one from a national election (picture C). The following three are pictures of the electronic device adopted in Salta

Source: All ballot copies come from the provincial and national electoral authorities. An electronic ballot simulator (pictures D to F) is https://simulador.electoralsalta.gob.ar/sufragio.html (accessed April 15, 2022)

Electronic Ballots

Figure 3 (cont.)

and place it in the same envelope.[3] Given this laborious process, voters may be less likely to cast a split ticket. But, when voters do cut their ballot, they may be less likely to re-engage with the ballot and more likely to rolloff. This is because not rolling off requires voters to physically locate the other ballot of choice and physically cut portions of the other party ballot to continue voting in the election.

The ballot also has clear implications for candidates – particularly those competing in down-ballot races. Since voters must physically split their ballot to vote for candidates from different parties, the fates of down-ballot candidates are literally tethered to the fates of top-of-the-ticket candidates. As we elaborate in Section 4, the physical design of the ballot, and consequently the reform we study in this Element, has clear implications for their electoral fortunes.

Finally, for political parties, this physical connection of candidates on the ticket limits small parties' ability to field candidates and win elections in down-ballot races. The partisan paper ballot places an enormous burden on individual political parties to print and distribute their own ballots, and monitor polling places to ensure their availability on election day – i.e., ensure they do not run out of ballots and their ballots are not stolen or damaged by their opponents. The burdens of printing and distributing ballots inform the campaign choices parties make and, consequently, their ability to cultivate supporters.

The Electronic Ballot

The electronic voting devices altered the voting routine in several ways. Salta's electronic vote, depicted in Figure 3D–F is composed of four basic elements: a touch-screen, a printer, a scanner, and a paper ballot. The voting process starts when the voter receives a paper ballot containing an electronic chip at the voting station. The ballot has no inscriptions and the chip holds no information. The voter inserts the ballot into the printer. Then, the voter approaches the touch screen as depicted in Figure 3D. She can choose to view the candidates sorted by elected positions, in which case the voter goes race by race, selecting the party she prefers for each office (Figure 3E); or by political party, in which case the voter can cast a straight ticket vote by selecting the preferred party in one single step (Figure 3F). In both cases, the ballot provides the option of voting blank for

---

[3] To cast a blank vote for the entire slate of candidates the voter has to place an empty envelope into the ballot box. But, if she wants to cast a blank ballot for only some of the categories at stake, the voter must physically split the ballot, place the portions of the ballot that she is expressing a preference over in the envelope, and omit the portions of the ballot for those she wants to cast the "blank" vote.

all or some races (bottom right corner of both images). Once the voter has finished making her choices, the voting machine prints the ballot, and the voter places it in the ballot box.

The reform makes several changes to the voting process, that have implications for representation. The new ballot structure eliminates the need to physically split the ticket, resulting in more ease and flexibility for voters who wish to vote for candidates from different political parties for the various offices at stake. After voters split their ticket, they can easily reengage with the ballot to cast a vote in the next contest, by simply advancing to the next screen. Voting in the next contest is no more physically demanding than voting blank or rolling off.

This ballot form also has implications for parties. As down-ballot candidates are not physically connected to-top-of-the-ballot candidates, it weakens party coattails in down-ballot elections. Under electronic voting, the electoral authority is charged with providing the devices and all the voting materials to the voting centers. Individual political parties are no longer responsible for the provision of ballots. Every party competing can count on a presence in every voting booth. As discussed in sections 5 and 6, this change has implications for how parties campaign across the state and which parties have a viable shot at winning a seat.

Although the adoption of electronic voting was simply designed to facilitate the administration of elections and improve voters' experience, the coming sections will show that it fundamentally changed the way voters vote, and consequently the strategic calculations and electoral payoffs for candidates and parties. This brief discussion provided the basic intuition about how replacing a partisan paper ballot with an electronic Australian ballot can affect voters, candidates, and parties. We develop the logic further and provide evidence for each of these claims in sections 3 to 6. Before turning to our evidence, we explain how we can use this reform to make inferences.

The Partial Rollout of Electronic Voting and Opportunities for Causal Inference

It can be difficult to draw causal inferences from institutional reforms. Most reforms happen all at once. Thus, even though there might be a clear before and after, because institutional reforms do not happen in a vacuum, it is hard to isolate the effect of a reform from other contextual factors that may be changing over the same time.

Moreover, the people who have the power to alter institutions are typically the same people who stand to benefit from the laws. Distributive models, the dominant explanation for electoral reform, argue that parties and politicians derive their preferences over institutional reforms by weighing whether they would get a competitive advantage from an alternative set of electoral rules. They seek to pass reform that secures their future political position (Remmer 2008). In Argentina, after the adoption of an electoral reform, incumbent governors controlling the reform process won about 8 percent more legislative seats than those expected by any other party with comparable vote shares (Calvo and Micozzi 2005). As some leaders may implement reforms in anticipation of a change in voter, candidate, or party behavior, it is difficult to rule out reverse causality.

Although we can never fully alleviate concerns with endogeneity associated with institutional reforms, there are several features of the ballot reform in Salta that strengthen our ability to draw causal inferences. First, electronic voting reform was implemented over the course of multiple elections. This partial rollout strategy allows us to treat the reform as a quasi-experiment.

Beyond this, elites do not always have complete control over the reform process, and other actors (e.g., voters and courts) may constrain the reformers' options (Renwick 2010). In Salta, despite the governor initiating the reform, the implementation was delegated to the Electoral Court and implemented by non-partisan actors. Consequently, we have fewer concerns that the reform was initially implemented in locations where the government foresaw an electoral benefit.

To elucidate these points, we next trace the history of the adoption and implementation of electronic voting in Salta. Then, we predict the partial implementation of electronic voting to show that bureaucratic concerns informed the initial placement of electronic voting machines, and political concerns were largely absent in this process. This informs our research design in subsequent sections – thus improving our ability to draw causal inferences about the effects of the electronic voting reform.

Incremental Implementation of Electronic Voting: A Bureaucratic Process

Electronic devices were incrementally implemented over five years. In 2007, the entire province used a partisan paper ballot. In 2008 the newly elected incumbent governor, Juan Manuel Urtubey, sent a bill to the Legislature that would allow the introduction of "new voting technologies" in provincial elections under the oversight of the Electoral Court. Later that year, the Legislature passed the reform (Law 7540). The Court was charged with deciding the location and scope of each stage of the implementation, the design of the electronic devices, and publicizing the new procedures.

The first stage of the rollout occurred in the 2009 primary and general elections. The Court conducted a small pilot comprising 10 voting booths in a single municipality, San Lorenzo, in the Peronist primaries. In-person surveys administered at the polling places indicated that voters were satisfied overall with the voting experience, motivating the Electoral Court to expand the use of electronic devices. The general election later that year hosted electronic devices in 36 booths distributed across six voting centers in the City of Salta and San Lorenzo (Page et al. 2016). The overall experience was viewed as a success, leading to a governor's decree establishing a timetable for the rest of the reform. In 2011, one third of registered voters would use electronic devices. By 2015, the entire province would vote using electronic devices (Decree 930/2010).

Prior to the 2011 election, the Electoral Court was responsible for designing and supplying the electronic ballots in consultation with political parties (Page et al. 2016). The Court presented the electronic devices to parties (*El Tribuno* December 2, 2010). With the parties' input, they determined design aspects such as the screen layout and the use of pictures and party logos (*El Tribuno* January 3, 2011, January 22, 2011). The Court also handled community relations, implementing training demonstrations for public officers and voters on the new voting devices in government local offices, community centers, and other local spots (*El Tribuno* September 14, 2010, January 29, 2011). Despite some complaints about the process being politicized (Page et al. 2016; Pomares et al. 2011), the implementation was largely concentrated in the hands of the Electoral Court.

Non-mandatory party primaries in 2011 offered another opportunity for an early test of the reform. A total of 325 electronic devices were used across three departments (*El Tribuno* January 3, 2011, January 19, 2011). For the general election, a few months later, the number of electronic devices was almost doubled. More than 700 machines were in place, to be used by half of the voters in the Capital Department, as well as different fractions of the voters in four other departments (*El Tribuno* February 6, 2011). In the 2011 general election, approximately one third of Salta voters cast their ballots electronically. Post-election surveys indicated that, although older voters and voters with lower levels of education faced relatively more difficulties, the vast majority of voters found the new procedure easy to use (Pomares et al. 2011).

Initially, Salta planned to extend electronic voting to two-thirds of the voters in the following election cycle, and later, to the entire province. However, the electoral authorities decided to speed up the implementation. Two years later (in the 2013 mid-term election), electronic devices were used throughout the entire

Table 1 Implementation of electronic voting over time, by type of election
Province of Salta, 2007–2019

2007	2009	2011	2013	2015	2017	2019
No implementation		**Partial implementation**	**Full implementation**			
All paper ballots		Some electronic some paper	All electronic voting			
Gov		Gov		Gov		Gov
Leg	Leg	Leg	Leg	Leg	Leg	Leg
Mayor		Mayor		Mayor		Mayor

Note: The abbreviations code the type of province- or local-level election by year in our dataset: *Gov*, Gubernatorial; *Leg*, Province House and Senate; *Mayor*, Mayoral and City Council

province. Since then, all province-level elections in Salta have used electronic voting. Table 1 summarizes the implementation of electronic voting in general elections in Salta. Throughout this Element, we draw on data from these seven election cycles, exploiting data of all gubernatorial, legislative, and mayoral elections, to draw inferences about the implications of the electronic voting reform.

The Initial Placement of Electronic Devices and a Quasi-Experimental Design

That electronic devices were partially implemented over the series of multiple elections under the control of bureaucrats improves our ability to draw causal inferences. The partial implementation of the reform in 2011 offers a unique opportunity to assess the impact of ballot structures on several outcomes of interest using a quasi-experimental design. A key feature of quasi-experiments is that they do not involve an explicit random assignment. In Salta, the partial implementation of the ballot reform required bureaucrats to make decision about where to pilot the devices. This may raise concerns that voting devices (during the partial roll-out) were initially placed in precincts where it is more likely to observe changes in outcomes of interests. To this end, we describe and systematically predict the initial placement of the electronic machines. We incorporate this information into our research designs in subsequent sections to improve our ability to draw causal inferences.

The province of Salta is divided into 23 departments, comprising 60 muni-cipalities. Many of these departments are mostly rural, thus most of the population lives in urban areas (83.9 percent, slightly behind the national average). Of the 1.4 million people living in the province according to 2022 census projections, almost a half live in the Capital Department, which hosts the City of Salta. No other city is larger than 100,000 people. The province is relatively poor in comparison to the national average. One-fifth of the households, according to census data, report unsatisfied basic needs – twice the national rate. The province's geography is relatively complex – warm low plains in the east with areas of thick jungle; cold high altitudes in the west, that includes a plateau three to four thousand meters above sea level; and valleys between them, where most of the population and economic activities are concentrated. This diverse geography adds to the logistical difficulties parties face when campaigning across the province.

Each municipality is divided into precincts, and electronic devices were assigned at this level. Every ballot box in a given precinct used the same voting procedure. As a result, the number of votes cast using electronic devices varied across departments (see Figure 4): (1) all voters kept partisan paper ballots in 18 departments; (2) two voting procedures were simultaneously in place in four departments; and (3) all voters cast their ballots using electronic devices in only one department (Cafayate). Overall, about 165,000 votes (29.5 percent) were cast using electronic machines.

The bulk of the implementation occurred in the Capital Department, the largest jurisdiction in the province, and home to almost a half of the

Votes casted with Electronic Devices (%, Province of Salta, 2011)

Geo-Location of Voting Centers using Electronic Devices (Capital Department, 2011)

Figure 4 Mapping the reform implementation in Salta

Note: One polling station that belongs to the same municipality and located in El Chamical, a rural area about 23 miles away from the city, is omitted from the Capital Department map

Source: Province of Salta's tile map by INDEC <www.indec.gob.ar/indec/web/ Institucional-Indec-Codgeo>. Capital Department's tile map by Stamen Design <http://maps.stamen.com/>, under CC BY 3.0, based on data by OpenStreetMap

provincial voters. 44.2 percent of the Capital Department's votes were cast using electronic devices. The first implementation of electronic voting also included a relatively large department, Orán, where 56.7 percent of the votes were cast with electronic devices; a middle-size jurisdiction, Metán (69.5 percent); and two small departments: Cafayate (100.0 percent) and La Caldera (34.5 percent).

The Capital Department comprises two municipalities: the City of Salta (i.e., the capital and the largest city in the province) and the much smaller Villa San Lorenzo. The City of Salta has 51 election precincts and 22 of them used electronic devices in 2011. Overall, the department is comprised of 54 election precincts. Each precinct hosted one to four polling places, and every polling place accommodated an average of ten voting booths. Electronic devices were somewhat more concentrated in the central and north areas of the city (see Figure 4, right panel). San Lorenzo only has three election precincts, and all of them used an electronic device in 2011.

What Factors Explain the Initial Placement of Electronic Voting Machines?

Once the choice of implementing the reform by precinct had been made, a second-order decision was the selection of the actual precincts where electronic devices were going to be piloted. The assignment criteria to the specific locations of the electronic devices were not random, but the rationale behind that decision was also not described to the public.

According to the national census (INDEC 2010), socioeconomic indicators vary considerably across and, to a lesser degree, within departments.[4] The Capital Department is the wealthiest jurisdiction in the province, presenting the highest levels of educational attainments and the lowest levels of structural poverty – only 18.8 percent of the households in the average election precinct were poor. Electoral precincts in General San Martín and Orán, departments rank second and third by population size, respectively 45.8 percent and 43.8 percent of the households in the average election precinct were poor. For comparison, 60.6 percent of the households in Rivadavia Department, the province's poorest jurisdiction, were living in poverty.

Bureaucratic motivations likely influenced the choice of where to pilot electronic devices. Elite interviews with the bureaucrats who organized the reform report that gradual implementation was a strategy to assure a successful execution and to avoid any resistance to the reform

---

[4] All the demographics throughout this Element rely on the 2010 census data, which is the closest data to the moment of the reform adoption.

(Pomares et al. 2014). More educated voters are expected to be more familiar with electronic devices, and thus, have fewer problems in their first experience with electronic voting. Thus, electronic devices were likely piloted in areas with higher levels of socioeconomic status and education (Pomares and Zárate 2014). A similar rationale seemed to have been adopted to assign electronic ballots in the 2009 primary election (Page et al. 2016): the pilot was conducted in a municipality significantly more urban and more educated than average.

> *Bureaucratic Hypothesis.* Electronic devices were more likely to be located in precincts with lower poverty and higher educational attainments.

There may have also been political motivations. Politics in Salta have been dominated by the Peronist Party since the end of the military dictatorship. Roberto Romero and Hernán Cornejo, both peronists, governed the province between 1983 and 1991, one term each. The Unión Cívica Radical (UCR) and the Partido Renovador de Salta (PRS) were the main opposition forces of relatively similar size. Roberto Ulloa, who had been the military governor in the 1970s and who was the founder of the PRS (Adrogué 1995), defeated the Peronist Party in 1991, becoming the only non-peronist governor in the entire period. The 1991 election was also a turning point for the UCR. The UCR finished in a very distant third place and was never competitive in the province again. Four years later, Juan Carlos Romero, son of the former governor, defeated the incumbent PRS and was elected for the first of three consecutive gubernatorial terms. Romero's success in the polls cemented the peronist dominance in the province.

The 2007 gubernatorial election marked the beginning of a new political cycle. Romero was term-limited and did not seek reelection as governor. Two different candidates with Peronist origins competed for the post. Walter Wayar, then three-term lieutenant governor, who had previously been a provincial senator and a provincial representative, ran under the label Frente Justicialista para la Victoria. He faced Juan Manuel Urtubey, a two-term House representative, and former cabinet member under the Romero's administration, who ran under the label Convergencia Salteña. Urtubey defeated Wayar in a tight election, 46.4 percent to 45.2 percent, winning the first of three consecutive gubernatorial terms, with the electoral support of the PRS.

There were significant regional disparities in Urtubey's electoral performance. He enjoyed a decisive victory in Metán and General San Martín departments where he won by 23.1 percent and 20.9 percent points, respectively, while losing in the departments of Iruya and Santa Victoria by 41.0 percent and 36.0 percent, respectively. The election results in the Capital Department, however, were much closer to the provincial average with Urtubey winning only by 1.3 points (44.3 percent to 43.0 percent).

Given that the governor spearheaded the decision to implement electronic voting and to do so incrementally, it is possible that political calculations guided the assignment of electronic devices. The adoption of a new voting procedure might disrupt territorial mobilization networks, hence risk-averse politicians would be expected to pilot the reform outside their electoral strongholds. And if that was their intention, implementing the ballot reform by election precinct would give them considerable flexibility to do it. They could carefully cherry-pick the areas where voters were going to use one procedure or the other.

> *Political Hypothesis.* Electronic devices were more likely to be located in precincts where the electoral support of the governor was weaker.

Systematically Predicting the Initial Placement of Electronic Voting Machines

To evaluate support for these expectations, we examine the implementation of electronic voting in the 2011 election. The treatment was assigned at the precinct level. Consequently, our unit of analysis is the electoral precinct. Our dependent variable codes whether a precinct was assigned electronic devices in 2011.

To test the Bureaucratic Hypothesis, we use measures of educational attainment and poverty from the 2010 census.[5] We reason that bureaucrats may assume educated people, and those with access to more resources, are more likely to have experience using electronic devices such as computers. This exposure would have been seen as valuable for facilitating the rollout of electronic voting. If the bureaucratic hypothesis is supported, we expect to observe a positive and significant relationship between education and the assignment of electronic devices, and a negative and significant relationship for poverty.

One challenge in developing our dataset is that demographic data is only available at the census tract level (INDEC 2010). Census tracts do not map on to electoral precincts. Rather, precincts may span across multiple tracts, including some complete tracts and portions of others. To address this measurement challenge, we built an original data set using ArcGIS to approximate the precinct boundaries based on the location of voting centers. This allows us to

---

[5] The level of educational attainment is measured as the percentage of the adult population who have a high-school education or higher. The poverty level is measured as the prevalence of structurally deficient households, which is a census-based measure of non-income poverty.

assign all of the census tracts to projected boundaries, creating measures of education and poverty for each precinct in Salta.[6]

To test the Political Hypothesis, we account for the share of the precinct that voted for the incumbent governor in the previous election. If the political hypothesis is supported, we anticipate a negative relationship between support for the incumbent governor and electronic voting.[7]

To assess whether the bureaucratic and political considerations affect the treatment assignment, we model the assignment of electronic ballots through a logistic model:

$$Pr(y_i = 1) = logit^{-1}(X_i\beta)$$

$$X_i\beta = \alpha + \beta_1 pov_i + \beta_2 educ_i + \beta_3 gov_i + \varepsilon_i$$

where i indexes the electoral precinct, the term y_i is a dummy variable that captures the type of voting procedure and it is coded '1' for electronic devices, β represents the coefficients capturing the effect of the X vector of demographic and electoral covariates on y_i, α is an intercept and ε_i is an error term for the ith observation. The X vector comprises precinct-level demographics as well as precinct-level electoral backgrounds. We evaluate our expectations on three different samples: the precincts located in the province capital, the interior precincts, and the entire province.

The results from this analysis support the Bureaucratic Hypothesis and not the Political Hypothesis. To begin, in support of the Bureaucratic Hypothesis, we observe a positive and significant relationship between education and the implementation of electronic voting. We do not, however, observe a significant relationship between poverty and the assignment of electronic voting once we control for education.

To illustrate the relationship between education and the assignment of electronic voting, Figure 5 presents the predicted probabilities of assigning electronic machines depending on the share of the educated population. The chances of piloting electronic voting significantly increase when the population is more educated. A precinct with 20 percent of its residents with complete high-school education (or higher) had about a 11.3 percent chance of voting using electronic devices, whereas a precinct with 40 percent of educated residents had more than a 63.2 percent chance. These differences are statistically significant.

---

[6] The Appendix II provides a detailed description of the construction of precinct boundaries.
[7] See Table II-2–1 in OA for three alternative samples: the entire province, the Capital Department, and the departments in the interior of the province.

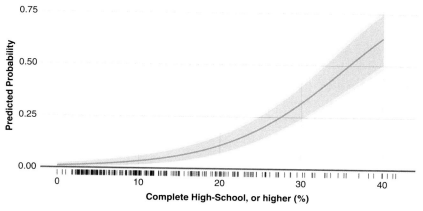

Figure 5 Predicted probability of piloting electronic voting, by level of education (90 percent and 95 percent C.I.), based on data from the Province of Salta (2011)

Note: Model predictions based on model 1, in Table II-2–1, in the Online Appendix (OA). Omitted variables, held at median values.

Importantly, we may think that education could also be a proxy for support for the Peronist Party. Education (and poverty) is associated with Peronist support (Calvo and Murillo 2019, 2004). The relationship between education and electronic ballot assignment holds even once controlling for poverty and support for the incumbent Peronist governor.

Turning to the Political Hypothesis, support for the incumbent governor is not negatively associated with the assignment of electronic voting. If anything, in some of our models, we observe a positive relationship. This is the opposite of what we would expect to observe if the placement of electronic ballots were politically motivated. Specifically, our models indicate that in the Capital Department, the chances of piloting electronic devices were not associated with Urtubey's election performance four years before. However, in the interior of the province, chances of assignment were larger in precincts with a larger electoral support for Urtubey.

Overall, this evidence suggests that reformers weighed the demographics characteristics of precinct when assigning electronic devices. But their considerations seemed to be guided by bureaucratic concerns and not political considerations.

Conclusions

The adoption of electronic voting in Salta, together with the adoption of paper-based Australian ballots in Córdoba and Santa Fe, brings rich innovations to the manner in which people vote. Such changes are not inconsequential though. This

Element is devoted to examining how voting procedures shape voting behavior as well as electioneering strategies. The findings in this section, combined with the unique partial-implementation of electronic voting across the province, serve as a foundation for addressing potential threats to our inferences.

We find evidence that bureaucratic concerns governed the implementation process. The anticipation of long lines, poorly informed ballot-box authorities, and confused voters concerned electoral authorities. It appears they attempted to head off these concerns by placing the first electronic voting machines in areas with more educated voters. We use the findings from this section to inform our research design in subsequent sections.

Despite that the initial mandate for electronic voting was handed down from the executive branch and passed by the Peronist majority in the assembly, the reform process, and its representational consequences, do not provide any evidence to suggest that political considerations guided the decision of where to pilot the first devices. From a micro-level perspective, the findings presented in this section indicate that the implementation of the reform was mostly driven by bureaucratic considerations. There is little to no evidence that the electronic devices were located in areas where the electoral bases of the governor were larger or slimmer. From a macro-level perspective, as we show in the next sections, the reform produced effects that did not benefit the incumbent party, such as weakening party coattails or helping opposition parties to penetrate its territorial fiefdoms.

3 Disconnecting Races: The Behavioral Implications of Independent Choices

In August 2011, Mauricio Macri, the mayor of Buenos Aires and leader of the political party Propuesta Republicana (PRO), announced the launch of his party's bid for the national election. Although the PRO was not fielding a presidential candidate, they hoped to secure seats in Congress. On the day of the public announcement, Mauricio Macri and congressman Federico Pinedo arrived at Las Heras Park to launch their campaign with massive scissors in hand (see Figure 6). The park was decorated with multicolored balloons and umbrellas. Party advocates distributed daisy-shaped brochures that read: "Don't cut the flowers, cut the ballot" (*Clarín* September 21, 2011).

From the onset, Macri and Pinedo called on their supporters to split their ballots, voting for the PRO in down-ballot races. As Pinedo explained: "One hundred percent of the citizens who want to vote for the PRO candidates are going to have to split the ballot and include the presidential candidate they want to vote for in the envelope, without the list of the House of Representatives from that party, and with the PRO's ballot instead" (*Ámbito Financiero* August 11,

Figure 6 National parties campaigning split-ticket voting: Propuesta
Republicana (2011)
Source: "El Jefe de Gobierno pidió el voto para su lista de Diputados en Capital: Macri
se metió en la pelea de octubre y llamó a cortar boleta." *Clarín*, September 21, 2011

2011).[8] Since the PRO was not fielding a presidential candidate, PRO supporters would require voters to cast a strategic vote – selecting a candidate from
a viable party for president and voting for their preferred party, the PRO, in
down-ballot races – or forgo voting in the presidential race all together.

Macri made a similar appeal to voters: "It is always good to have balance, so
that not everything is [controlled by] one person. Our list goes by itself and we
require an effort: that people cut ballots and support this stellar list" (*Clarín*
September 21, 2011).[9] One of the nation's leading newspapers, *Clarín*, predicted:
"the word 'balance' will be heard often from the PRO leadership during this
campaign" (*Clarín* September 21, 2011).[10] Between Macri and Pinedo, the PRO
campaign touched on two classic motivations for split-ticket voting: strategic

---

[8] Original quote: "Nosotros tenemos un problema, o mejor dicho, una dificultad en la próxima
elección del 14 de agosto y es que presentamos una boleta para diputados sin candidato
a Presidente", dijo Pinedo, en declaraciones al programa "Bajo la Lupa", que se emite por FM
Identidad de esta Capital. "Es decir, el 100 por ciento de los ciudadanos que quieran votar a los
candidatos del PRO van a tener que cortar boleta e incluir en el sobre al candidato presidencial
que quieran votar, sin la lista a diputados de esa agrupación y con la boleta del PRO en su lugar",
indicó (*Ámbito Financiero* August 11, 2011). www.ambito.com/politica/pinedo-tenemos-una-
dificultad-ir-candidato-presidente-n3695274 (accessed May 26, 2022).

[9] Original quote: "Siempre es bueno tener equilibrio, que no todo esté en una sola persona. Nuestra
lista va solita y requerimos un esfuerzo: que la gente corte boleta y apoye esta lista de lujo"
(*Clarín* September 21, 2011). www.clarin.com/politica/Macri-octubre-llamo-cortar-
boleta_0_r1SG00hhvme.html (accessed May 26, 2022).

[10] Original quote: "La palabra 'equilibrio' se escuchará seguido en el desfile de dirigentes de PRO"
(*Clarín* September 21, 2011). www.clarin.com/politica/Macri-octubre-llamo-cortar-
boleta_0_r1SG00hhvme.html (accessed May 26, 2022).

voting (Blombäck and de Fine Licht 2017; Cox 1997; Moser and Scheiner 2009) and ideological/partisan balancing (Burden and Helmke 2009).

Regardless of voters' motivations to split their ballot, the design of voting procedures can discourage split-ticket voting. As we illustrated in Section 2, splitting the partisan paper ballot used across most of Argentina is a very involved process. Thus, it is not surprising that the PRO felt it was necessary to run an aggressive campaign focused on cutting the ballot. Some voters may prefer to split their vote, but they may not always be willing to pay the costs associated with splitting their ticket, especially when complicated ballot structures create obstacles to doing so (Burden and Kimball 2002; Engstrom and Kernell 2014; Rusk 1970). Evidently, the PRO was keenly aware of this challenge. As Pinedo explained it: "many people do not like" cutting the ballot, despite the fact that it is a "simple procedure."

In fact, in this section we show that needing scissors to split your ballot can be a major deterrent. And, once voters cut their ballot, they may be less likely to re-engage with the ballot and more likely to roll-off. By contrast, we show that more user-friendly ballot structures such as the electronic Australian ballot, that allow voters to split their ballot by simply ticking different boxes, encourage voters to cast votes for different parties. Equally important, once voters split their ballot, we find that they are less likely to roll-off when using the electronic Australian ballot, then when using the traditional partisan paper ballot.

The Consequences of Voting Procedures and Ballot Structures on the Choices of Voters

Voters are frequently called upon to make multiple decisions for different contests in the same election. In presidential democracies, national legislators are often elected on the same day of the presidential election. Different levels of government (e.g., presidents and governors) are commonly elected on the same day. In such cases, straight-ticket voting is the dominant form of voting.

Split-ticket voting, wherein voters cast a vote for a different party for different contests in the same election, is a common feature in many elections (Campbell and Miller 1957). Voters may split their ballot to produce ideological or partisan balance, to support candidates who exhibit desirable personal traits, or to avoid wasting their vote by voting strategically (Cox 1997; Blombäck and de Fine Licht 2017; Burden and Helmke 2009; Moser and Scheiner 2009). Regardless of voters' motivations, the more they split their ballot, the more races for different elected offices become independent of one another. In presidential systems, the degree of connectedness or independence influences the distribution of legislative seats and subsequently, which voters, policies, and preferences are represented in office.

Rates of split-ticket voting vary substantially across political and institutional contexts. In the United States, for instance, splitting the ticket between presidential and House elections rose from about 12 percent of the voters in the 1950s, to more than 25 percent during the 1980s. It declined again in the 1990s (Burden and Kimball 2002). These values vary across congressional districts, depending in part on how contested the election is (Burden and Kimball 2002). Split-ticket voting tends to be higher in countries with multiparty competition and weakly institutionalized parties (Moser and Scheiner 2009). In Mexico, by comparison, where there are far fewer competitive political parties, less than 10 percent of voters split their ballot during concurrent presidential elections (Helmke 2009). Ticket-splitting in mixed-member electoral institutions also varies substantially, ranging from a low of 8.73 percent in Hungary to more than 30 percent in New Zealand and South Korea (Rich 2014).

Even when voters have an incentive to split their ticket, ballot forms influence the cost of doing so. The manner in which candidates are presented on the ballot affects the centrality of parties and consequently, the likelihood of splitting the vote. Ballots that reinforce party-centric information cues, such as party name or logo, are linked to more straight-ticket voting (Calvo et al. 2009; Engstrom and Kernell 2014; Katz et al. 2011; Rusk 1970; Tchintian 2018). And, when ballots do not offer a straight party option, splitting one's vote is no more costly than voting straight-ticket (Walker 1966; Darcy and Schneider 1989).

Ballot structures vary in terms of the cognitive and physical demands they place on voters. Some ballots require voters to select or punch multiple boxes, to cut or tear the ballot, or to use complex machines that demand considerable attention. Such variation in ballot structure informs voters' behavior at the polls, affecting their likelihood of casting a split-ticket vote. Even when voters prefer to split their ticket, the costs imposed by complicated ballot structures may be sufficient to discourage voters from doing so. By contrast, other ballot structures streamline the ticket-splitting process, making it easy for motivated voters to split their votes. When voters can split their ballot without incurring any additional costs, they are more likely to do so, even if they do not anticipate it will result in clear electoral payoffs.

Although this logic is general, we focus on the implications of the ballot reform introduced in Section 2. The partisan paper ballots, previously used in Salta, Argentina, are a good example of how the ballot structure can discourage split-ticket voting. To vote straight-ticket all voters need to do is select a ballot, put it in an envelope, and place it in the ballot box. Hence, straight-ticket voting is the most easy and convenient choice. Split-ticket voting, instead, requires voters to manually tear a paper ballot, demanding extra effort and time at the ballot box. By contrast, streamlined voting procedures such as the Australian ballot simplify the vote-splitting process. Voters only need to click a button or check a box to choose executive and legislative candidates from different parties. We thus posit:

> *Split-ticket Voting Hypothesis.* The average level of split-ticket voting will be lower with the partisan paper ballots than with the Australian ballot.

Ballot design may also influence how often voters roll off (Stewart 2011). Recall, ballot roll-off is the phenomenon where voters cast a valid vote for races at the top of the ticket but not for offices further down the ballot. On some ballots, roll-off may be achieved by skipping over a specific race or contest, as in the United States, or by removing that portion of the ballot altogether, as is the case for the Argentine partisan paper ballot. Other ballot structures may require voters to actively select an option to vote blank or "voto en blanco," as it appears on the ballots used in some Latin American countries and on the electronic ballot in Salta.

Voters may intentionally avoid casting a vote for down-ballot races, as a result of lack of interest/information or even as a protest vote (Barnes and Rangel 2018; Driscoll and Nelson 2014). Alternatively, roll-off may result from voter fatigue or unintentional errors. High levels of ballot roll-off have implications for electoral outcomes, representation, and democratic legitimacy (Bowler and Donovan 2000; Sinclair and Alvarez 2004). In general, the same factors that explain overall levels of political participation (e.g., interests, information, and demographics) also explain why some voters intentionally abstain from down-ballot races (Barnes and Rangel 2014, 2018; Lamb and Perry 2020; Wattenberg et al. 2000).

Importantly, research also indicates that under-voting might be linked to voting procedures. In his 1966 study, Walker pointed out that some ballot designs significantly increase roll off due to voter fatigue: "The more complex the design of the ballot, the greater the tendency for voters to neglect races at the bottom of the ticket" (p. 462). Subsequent research has provided more evidence that ballot form may induce voter fatigue or even voter confusion (Bowler et al. 1992; Caltech/MIT 2001; Darcy and Schneider 1989). In this vein, a specific set of voting procedures – such as lever machines, optical scanned ballots, and electronic voting machines – has been associated with different rates of ballot roll-off (Ansolabehere and Stewart 2005).

In the case of Argentina, the partisan paper ballot disengages voters who split the ballot. After cutting their ballot, to continue voting for down-ballot offices, a voter needs to start the process again: identify the ballot corresponding to the party she prefers, manually cutting a second ballot, and placing the corresponding pieces in the envelope. Every time a voter splits the ticket, the cost of voting for a lower office increases. Some voters may opt to abstain from down-ballot elections, rather than engaging in this elaborate process.

The electronic devices, by contrast, offer voters the option to easily split their votes without rolling off. If, on the one hand, voters choose to view the ballot arranged by a political party, they can easily cast a straight-ticket ballot and avoid any roll-off. If, on the other hand, they choose to view their ballot arranged by elected position, voters are required to move through the ballot contest-by-contest, selecting a party for each office at stake. If they choose not to vote for a given contest, they still have to select the option to vote blank. The process of rolling off is the same as the process required to cast a vote. Every time voters split the vote, they are automatically re-engaged in the voting process: the next screen will present them the choices for the next office. Compared to the partisan paper ballots, it makes it simpler to continue voting in down-ballot races. Hence, we posit:

> *Ballot Roll-off Hypothesis.* The average level of ballot roll-off will be higher under the partisan paper ballots than under the electronic ballot.

Leveraging an Incremental Ballot Reform: A Quasi-Experiment

Given that the same politicians who stand to benefit from different ballot structures are also typically responsible for selecting and implementing ballots, studies of ballot reform are rife with concerns about endogeneity. A number of factors such as candidate quality, polarization, and the strength of partisan attachments may influence both a politician's incentives to implement ballot reform and voters' decisions to split their ballot and/or roll-off. And yet, these factors can be difficult to observe and measure.

To alleviate some concerns associated with endogeneity, we leverage a quasi-experimental design, exploiting the incremental implementation of the reform. This research design allows us to test the effect of the ballot structure within a single election while holding a number of confounding factors constant. We develop a quasi-experimental design, by analyzing data from three elections where gubernatorial and provincial legislative elections were held concurrently.[11] In the 2007 election, all voters used partisan paper ballots

---

[11] A similar identification strategy has been employed to examine ballot effects by Nicolau 2015; Zucco and Nicolau 2016; and Barnes et al. 2017.

(no implementation). In 2011, a portion of the voters used electronic devices (partial implementation) and everyone else continued with the paper ballots. In 2015 every voter cast their ballot using the electronic device (full implementation). The incremental ballot reform occurred within a single district, the Capital Department, such that all voters voted in the exact same election, for the same contests, and were presented with the same candidate options.

The unit of analysis – also the unit of assignment for the treatment condition – is the electoral precinct. There are 54 precincts in the Capital District. Precincts using electronic devices in the 2011 election are the "treatment group." Precincts using paper ballots in the 2011 election are the "control group."

Treatments in quasi-experiments do not involve an explicit random assignment (Gerber and Green 2012). This is the primary feature of our research design that distinguishes it from a natural experiment. The bureaucrats and politicians responsible for the treatment assignment did not make their criteria known. Our empirical analysis in Section 2 indicates that electronic devices were more likely to be assigned to precincts with higher socioeconomic status. We also have reason to believe that political concerns may have influenced the treatment criteria. To address these potential threats to random assignment, we match precincts from the treatment and control group over a set of observable socio-demographic and political characteristics.[12]

Matching is a method for preprocessing observational data to improve causal inferences. The goal is to construct a dataset where background conditions in the sample are balanced (and ideally, equal) across the treatment and control groups, before conducting the parametric analysis. This approach allows us to account for the potential confounding effects between the treatment and the outcome variables, and it reduces the probability that the results are model dependent (Ho et al. 2007). We employ Coarsened Exact matching to reconstruct the balance in the sample (King and Nielsen 2019; Iacus et al. 2012). We use two alternative matching thresholds: the stricter threshold creates a more balanced post-matching sample at the cost of reducing the sample size. Model results do not differ significantly due to the selected threshold.[13]

---

[12] Other factors – such as poverty and incumbent party support – might also influence the assignment. Data was matched over these three covariates – the percentage of the precinct's population with complete high-school education or higher, the percentage of the precinct's population with unsatisfied basic needs, and the electoral support of the incumbent governor in the election before the reform adoption.

[13] Table II-3-1, in the OA, reports the balance improvements after matching the precincts. The use of matching methods significantly reconstructed the sample balance: improvement goes from 79.6 percent for poverty rate, to 90.1 percent for incumbent's vote share.

We use a standard DiD approach to examine the causal relationship between ballot form and split-ticket voting and roll-off using the matched sample.[14] In the typical DiD specification, there are only two periods – before and after. However, our data has three observation points, no implementation (2007), partial implementation (2011), and full implementation (2015). Consequently, we conduct two DiD analyses: the first comparing the no implementation period to partial implementation, and the second comparing the partial implementation to the full implementation.

$$y_{it} = split_{it} \sim N\left(X_{it}\beta, \sigma^2\right)$$

$$X_{it}\beta = \alpha + \beta_T T + \beta_A A + \delta(T * A)$$

Each observation in the data is an election precinct. The term $split_{it}$ is the split-ticket voting in the precinct i in the period t. The term T is a dummy variable that captures possible differences between the treatment and control groups prior to the reform adoption: $T = 1$ for the treated group. The term A is a time period dummy that captures aggregate factors that would cause changes in vote splitting even in the absence of a ballot change: $A = 1$ for the after period. The coefficient δ is the DiD estimator.

In sum, the precinct-level analysis combined with partial implementation allows us to examine different ballot structures applied in the exact same district, in the exact same election (i.e., the same candidates), under the same electoral rules. This is the primary advantage of a within-election analysis – that is, it facilitates a controlled comparison across precincts where other potentially confounding factors are held constant. For causal identification, this design is superior to a cross-sectional design wherein institutional and political factors vary substantially, making it more difficult to isolate the effect of the ballot form. The rest of the section examines election data from these three cycles in the Capital Department.

The Influence of the Ballot Structure on Split-Ticket Voting

Split-ticket voting varies considerably across precincts and over time in Salta. Precincts with the highest levels of split-ticket voting showed rates about three times larger than other precincts. On average, the share of split ballots was higher in precincts using electronic devices than in those using the ballot-and-envelope

---

[14] Table II-3–2, in the OA, reports the pre-matching and post-matching sample sizes. As expected, the stricter threshold produces a larger reduction of the sample but a better balance between control and treatment groups.

system.[15] In fact, in 2011, the fifteen precincts with the most split-ticket voting all used electronic devices. By contrast, almost all of the precincts with the least split tickets used paper ballots. There is a clear jump in the share of split ballots between the control and treatment precincts in 2011. Importantly, there is no clear pattern between levels of ballot splitting and ballot design in the other two elections, when voting procedures were the same.

The DiD analysis, comparing the 2007 election (no electronic voting) to the 2011 election (partial implementation),[16] shows that the average share of split ballots between the executive and legislative election was 9.10 percent in the control group, and 9.53 percent in the treatment group. The analysis shows that in 2011 the difference was substantially larger. Whereas the share of vote splitting was only 5.67 percent in precincts with paper ballots, the share of split ballots was about double in precincts with electronic devices to 10.22 percent. The DiD comparison between 2007 and 2011 provides strong evidence of the ballot effect: overall, the adoption of electronic voting corresponds to a statistically significant increase of 4.13 percentage points.

Four years later, once electronic devices were implemented in all precincts, differences between precincts entirely disappeared. This provides additional evidence for the influence of voting procedures on individual behavior. Whereas the partial implementation resulted in a two-fold increase in ballot splitting between treatment and control groups, the share of split ballots is statistically indistinguishable between the same precincts in 2015, when all precincts used electronic voting: 7.66 and 7.94 percent, in treatment and control groups, respectively.

Figure 7 presents the predicted differences between treated and control precincts in each election cycle. The share of split ballots in 2007 and 2015, when voters used the same voting procedure, is statistically indistinguishable between the treatment and control groups. Instead, when two voting procedures were in place, there was a significant difference across precincts: +4.56 percent. If some idiosyncratic, unobserved characteristics of the voters in the precincts where electronic devices were implemented were driving the results, similar differences would be expected to emerge in the two remaining elections. On the contrary, we observe no such patterns, indicating that

---

[15] The dependent variable measures the overall share of split tickets by precinct. To calculate the share of split ballots within a precinct, $split_i$, we take the absolute value of the difference in the gubernatorial candidate's votes, G_{ip}, compared to the legislative ticket's votes, D_{ip}, for each party p competing in each precinct i. We sum across all parties in precinct i, divide by two and weigh the value as a share of the total valid votes, V_i, in the precinct.

[16] Table II-3–3, in the OA, reports the results of the difference-in-differences analysis of split-ticket voting for the 2007 election (no electronic voting), the 2011 election (partial implementation), and the 2015 election (full implementation).

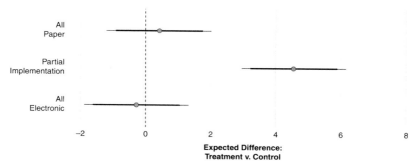

Figure 7 Predicted vote-splitting difference by treatment group (90 percent and 95 percent C.I.), based on data from the Capital Department (2007–2015)

Note: Model predictions based on difference-in-differences analysis, in Table II-3–3, in the OA.

differences between precincts observed in the partial implementation are attributable to the voting procedure.

Still, it is important to note that even though electronic voting is associated with an increase in split-ticket voting within the exact same election, the overall levels of split-ticket voting decreased between the 2007 (no implementation) and 2015 (full implementation) elections. To understand the difference in the overall level of split-ticket voting between different elections, it is necessary to consider the larger political context: the overall level of split-ticket voting is a function of many factors. In the case of Salta, split-ticket voting was likely higher in 2007 because of a more competitive gubernatorial election and a larger number of parties fielding candidates. Competitiveness and fragmentation are both associated with increases in split-ticket voting (Burden and Kimball 2002). Whereas Urtubey was elected governor in 2007 by a narrow margin (1.1 percent), he was reelected in 2011 and 2015 by a difference of more than 20 points over the runner-up. Moreover, ten political parties fielded gubernatorial candidates in 2007, compared to only eight in 2011 and five in 2015.

The Influence of the Ballot Structure on Roll-Off

In every election, there are a number of voters that turn out but do not cast a vote in every contest at stake. There are two common measures that scholars use to study this phenomenon: residual votes, and ballot roll-off. Residual votes measure votes cast in a given race relative to overall level of turnout; whereas ballot roll-off measures the relationship between the votes cast for a candidate at the top of the ticket compared to those in down-ballot races. We look first at residual votes to establish a baseline expectation for how many voters do not cast a ballot in a given race. Then we turn to ballot roll-off.

First, we measure residual votes as the percentage of people who turned out and did not cast a vote for any candidate. Residual votes vary significantly across offices. Voters are often more interested in the election of executive offices, hence it is not surprising that there are fewer residual votes in the gubernatorial race than in the legislative or mayoral races. Residual votes vary across time as well. The average rate in the gubernatorial election at the Capital Department was 5.1 in 2007; it fell to less than a half, 2.2, four years later; and grew again to 3.4 in the last election cycle. Such variations across offices and across time are fairly common elsewhere (see Ansolabehere and Stewart 2005).

Residual votes may vary across races and time depending on office saliency and quality of the pool of candidates, but they may also differ within the same election: descriptive data shows that some precincts may present five or six times more residual votes than others. Differences between treatment and control precincts in the implementation year were, however, significantly above average. Before the implementation of electronic voting, the average of residual votes was roughly the same for the two groups: 4.86 percent in the control group, and 4.09 percent in the treatment group. In 2011, the difference between groups was much larger. Whereas residual votes were only 1.61 percent in precincts with paper ballots, the average increased almost twofold in precincts with electronic devices to 3.20 percent.

To further assess this relationship, we use the same DiD research design that we adopted to examine split ticket voting. In this analysis the dependent variable is residual votes.[17] Consistent with our expectations, the DiD comparison between 2007 and 2011 indicates that the adoption of electronic voting corresponds to a statistically significant increase of 2.36 percentage points. When all the precincts used electronic voting in the following election, differences between groups were not significant.

Ballot roll-off is the difference of votes cast between the office at the top of the ticket and down-ballot races, and it measures the number of voters that express a preference in the most important race but abstained from casting a vote in some or all the down-ballot races. Figure 8 shows the average residual votes for province- and local-level races between 2007 and 2015.[18] Roll-off in

---

[17] Table II-3–4, in the OA, reports the results of the difference-in-differences analysis of ballot roll-off for gubernatorial elections, in the 2007 election (no electronic voting), the 2011 election (partial implementation), and the 2015 election (full implementation).

[18] Voters cannot split their ticket between the mayoral race and the city council race. As such the results for city council roll-off are, by definition, the same as the results for mayoral roll-off.

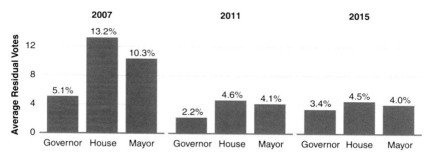

Figure 8 Average residual votes, by office and year (Capital Department, 2007–2015)

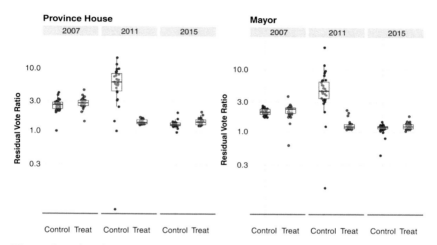

Figure 9 Ratio of residual votes, by implementation stage and treatment group (Capital Department, 2007-2015)

province House and mayoral elections, as it is clear in the figure, was significant in the first election cycle, but much smaller in the following two renovations. Of those who turned out in 2007, 13.2 percent did not vote for any party in the province House election. Engagement in the mayoral election was higher, but still the residual vote rate was 10.3 percent. Instead, in the next two elections, residual votes in House and mayoral elections remained between 4.0 and 4.6 percent.

Figure 9 illustrates the influence of the voting procedure on ballot roll-off. It presents the ratio of down-ballot residual votes over those in the gubernatorial election, by year and group. A ratio of 1 represents a precinct where residual votes in the gubernatorial race were the same as in the corresponding down-ballot competition, either the legislative or the mayoral election. The ratio rises

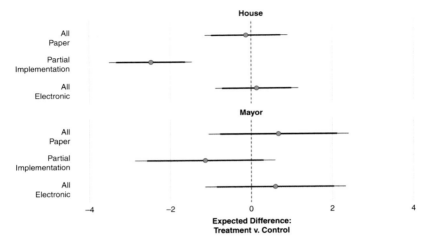

Figure 10 Predicted ballot roll-off difference by treatment group (90 percent and 95 percent C.I.), based on data from the Capital Department (2007–2015)

Note: Model predictions based on difference-in-differences analysis, in Table II-3–5, in the OA.

above 1 when there were more residual votes in the down-ballot race than in the gubernatorial election; and it falls below 1 when there were more votes for candidates in down-ballot offices. The y-axis is logged to keep the symmetry in the representation of the ratio values.

To begin, there are no meaningful differences between precincts when all the voters used the same ballot form, both in 2007 and in 2015, for both legislative and mayoral elections. By contrast, the ratio of residual votes was significantly higher among voters in the control group, i.e., using paper ballots, in the partial implementation year; and this was true for both offices. In a nutshell, voters were more frequently engaged in down-ballot races when using electronic devices than when using partisan paper ballots. This pattern holds despite that the saliency of the election and the quality of the pool of candidates were exactly the same.

Figure 10 presents the differential effect of electronic voting on treatment versus the control precincts based on the DiD research design. It shows two sets of results, one on the election of the provincial representatives, and the other on the election of mayors.[19] Ballot roll-off has been overall larger in House elections, which means that it is the office that voters most frequently skipped

---

[19]   Table II-3–5, in the OA, reports the results of the difference-in-differences analysis of ballot roll-off for House and mayoral elections, in the 2007 election (no electronic voting), the 2011 election (partial implementation), and the 2015 election (full implementation).

over on the ballot. However, ballot roll-off was roughly the same in 2007 across all precincts: 8.33 percent in the control group, and 8.20 percent in the treatment group. Yet, in 2011, the difference between groups was significantly larger. Whereas roll-off was 3.62 percent in precincts with paper ballots, the average roll-off was about a third in precincts voting with electronic devices: only 1.14 percent. The DiD comparison between 2007 and 2011 indicates that the adoption of electronic voting corresponds to a statistically significant decrease in roll-off of about 2.35 percentage points. Instead, when all the precincts used electronic voting in the 2015 election, differences disappeared entirely. Ballot roll-off was 1.20 and 1.06 percent in treatment and control groups, respectively, a statistically indistinguishable difference.

The overall level of ballot roll-off is lower in mayoral elections; in practice, this means that a portion of voters often skips the House election – which is the race immediately following the gubernatorial ticket – but after that, voters reengage and vote in the local election. The DiD analysis suggests that the same treatment effect is observed in mayoral elections. In 2011, roll-off was 1.92 percent in precincts with paper ballots, while the average roll-off was 0.79 percent in precincts voting with electronic devices. The relationship is, however, statistically weaker than for House elections.

Together, the DiD analyses provide strong support for our hypothesis that the ballot form affects the ability of voters to express their political preferences. The number of residual votes in the gubernatorial election increased in elections using electronic devices. More importantly, the new voting procedures require voters to continue engaging in down-ballot races whether they choose to vote blank or select a candidate competing in a down ballot contest. This is reflected in how the number of residual votes in down-ballot races, as a proportion of the residual votes at the top of the ticket, became much smaller in precincts voting with electronic devices. It is evident from the 2007–2011 comparison that the implementation of electronic voting significantly increased ballot roll-off in House elections, and to a lesser degree, in mayoral races. The 2011–2015 comparison, moreover, makes clear that the differences were not due to some idiosyncratic characteristic of the precincts, but instead are due to the voting procedures.

Conclusions

Voting procedures can affect the behavior of voters, and consequently, the election outcomes. Ballot designs differ in terms of the cognitive and physical demands they place on voters. There is evidence that features such as ballot length (Wattenberg et al. 2000), the order and placement of parties and candidates (Ho and Imai 2008; Miller and Krosnick 1998), and the inclusion of informational cues (Moehler and Conroy-Krutz 2016) can inform voters satisfaction with the voting, their trust in the election, and their voting behavior. The findings in this section contribute to this research by showing that voting procedures affect voters' choices.

Our results demonstrate how different ballot structures, within the exact same electoral institutions, can transform the electoral environment from one where voters are effectively discouraged from splitting their votes to one where voters are able to deliberately maximize their interests by more accurately translating their preferences at the polls, undermining the coattails of the candidates at the top of the ticket. Consequently, the electronic ballot would make it easier for voters to split their ticket supporting different parties in the executive and legislative races – just as the PRO was campaigning for its supporters to do when they showed up in Las Heras Park with giant cartoon scissors.

Additionally, our results demonstrate how the voting procedures affect the participation of voters in down-ballot races, either increasing or reducing the costs of reengaging with the ballot. The strength of the quasi-experimental design employed in this section is that it allows us to isolate the effect of the voting procedure from the idiosyncratic characteristics of precinct constituencies, from candidate quality, and from the electoral environment of each election cycle, permitting a more precise estimate of the ballot effect.

These findings have important implications for how representation linkages operate in democracies. The influence of the ballot form on vote splitting affects legislative elections, shaping presidential coattails (Engstrom and Kernell 2014) and incumbency advantage (Carson and Roberts 2013). A closer connection of executive and legislative elections is associated with fewer legislative parties and larger chances of a legislative majority backing the president's agenda (Cox 1997; Shugart and Carey 1992). This may facilitate the policy-making process and reduce the likelihood of legislative gridlock. By contrast, a ballot structure that facilitates ballot splitting, weakens the link between the executive and the legislature. Although less efficient for policy making, it may manufacture more inclusive legislative outcomes, demanding bigger efforts from the executive to construct majorities in the assembly. At the same time, large rates of ballot roll-off suggest a significant portion of the electorate fails to participate in low-profile elections, weakening the representativeness of down-ballot offices. A ballot form that reduces undervoting in provincial and local races, as the adopted electronic voting did, may reinvigorate the democratic connection of the elected officials with voters.

Importantly, the effect of ballots does not end at the ballot box. The ballot forms affect the electoral opportunities of candidates and the electioneering strategies of parties. In the next section we examine the implications of the ballot reform for individual candidates.

4 The Rise of the Personal Vote: The Implications for Candidates

When "ConVocación por San Isidro," a party competing in local elections in a suburb of Buenos Aires, was first starting off, they ran alongside a national party in an effort to attract more votes to their ballot. Even though they did not themselves field a candidate in the presidential or gubernatorial election, they knew that without a strong candidate at the top of the ticket the likelihood of winning many votes was slim: races at the top of the ticket structure electoral competition in down-ballot races. But, in 2011, ConVocación decided to go at it alone, despite the strength of top-of-the-ticket coattails.

Addressing this challenge head on, ConVocación started to actively campaign for voters to split their ballot – voting for ConVocación in down-ballot races. Flyers describing how to split a ballot were handed out in the streets and dropped in mailboxes (see Figure 11). They were not shy about explaining to voters that they could simultaneously vote for ideologically close parties at the top of the ballot. Party volunteers assembled tables on the street to canvas neighbors and passersby. They displayed two-meter tall cardboard scissors at each side of the table, visually reminding voters to cut their ballot. Candidates frequently appear in campaign pictures holding oversized scissors in their hands. And this double entendre was even incorporated into the party slogans – "Cortá con lo que ya fue" (Cut with the past) – asking voters to figuratively leave the past behind, by literally cutting their ballot. By most accounts, this campaign effort was successful as they captured upwards of 20 percent of the votes in 2011, and then won two to three council seats in every election cycle between 2013 and 2021.

The disproportionate emphasis on cutting the ballot for local parties is necessary in the Argentine context because the partisan paper ballot reinforces coattails. Other ballot structures make it easier to split the vote. When party coattails become less important, down-ballot races can disassociate their campaign from the top of the ticket and focus on the personal reputation of candidates. In the case of ConVocación, as well as other parties in a similar position, such ballots would perhaps allow them to center their campaign on candidates and local issues in the election. As such, weakened coattails make it easier for candidates competing in down-ballot races to cultivate a personal vote.

Figure 11 Local parties campaigning split-ticket voting: ConVocación por San Isidro (2017, 2021)

In this section, we investigate whether this is the case. Specifically, we argue that personal vote-earning attributes may be more important for garnering votes under some ballot forms. We leverage data from mayoral elections in Salta to focus on two candidate-level features: experience and gender.

Ballot Structure, Split-Ticket Voting, and the Fate of Down-Ballot Candidates

Mayoral races are generally listed down the ballot, after national- and province-level offices. Voters typically lack information about candidates competing further down the ballot (Atkeson and Hamel 2020; Holman and Lay 2021). As a result, the electoral fates of candidates competing in down-ballot races are heavily influenced by coattails from offices at the top – i.e., voters choose candidates in down-ballot races who are competing under the same party as their preferred candidates at the top of the ballot. Hence, if a mayoral candidate competes on the ticket of a party with a large electoral base or on a ballot with popular candidates at the top, they are likely to attract more votes than if the same candidate competes on a ticket with a small party or under an unpopular candidate.

Still, the extent to which electoral coattails influence the electoral fortunes of candidates varies dramatically depending on the ballot structure. When straight-ticket voting is the norm, the fates of candidates further down the ballot are largely dependent on the success of the candidates at the top – that is, the coattail effect. By contrast, the electronic ballot adopted in Salta, as shown in Section 3, resulted in a large uptick in split-ticket voting. Ballot designs encourage voters to make independent choices for each contest at stake, facilitate split-ticket voting, and ultimately reduce the saliency of coattails. Consequently, candidates in down-ballot races do not benefit as much from the strength of the candidate at the top of the ticket. Voters may be less likely to simply extend their party choice to all races down the ballot, opting instead to make discrete decisions for each race. If so, personal vote-earning attributes and other information cues may become more salient for candidates competing down the ballot.

Conventionally, personal vote refers to "that portion of a candidate's electoral support which originates in his or her personal qualities, qualifications, activities, and record" (Cain et al. 1987: 9). Although there is a wide range of individual attributes that can affect the fate of candidates, we focus on two individual features that we can systematically observe in our data: experience and gender. Based on records from the Electoral Court, we recorded the incumbency status, experience in the province legislature, and the gender of each candidate competing in the 2007–2019 mayoral elections. We leverage this information to examine how the ballot form interacts with the experience and gender of mayoral candidates.

The Influence of Careers: Amplifying the Incumbency Bonus

Individuals with prior career experience may develop resources that are useful when running for office. Of particular interest, political experience helps individuals to develop name recognition, political connections, and party networks, which aid candidates in their bid for election. In this section, we focus on two forms of political experience: incumbency status and experience as a provincial legislator.[20]

---

[20] We limit our analysis to this type of experience because it is virtually impossible to track down systematic information on non-political careers of candidates competing for local-level elections

Incumbents are powerful candidates (Gelman and King 1990; Patty et al. 2019). In addition to name recognition, incumbents enjoy considerable media attention and significant organizational resources. Once they join any race, they are almost always included in the pool of viable candidates. As a matter of fact, data from 240 mayoral elections in Salta indicates that incumbent mayors outperform non-incumbents by between 29 and 32 points.[21]

Just over half of the advantage is typically attributed to the personal vote factors such as name recognition, experience in office, and interactions with voters through casework (Trounstine 2011). The remaining bonus is attributed to partisanship and the political environment such as current political issues (Mustillo and Polga-Hecimovich 2020). The extent to which any of these factors benefit incumbents on the election day varies depending on a number of important political and institutional features (Desposato and Petrocik 2003).

We reason that the personal vote should be more important when candidates compete on ballots that facilitate split-ticket voting. In this circumstance, candidates benefit more from their own personal reputation than in elections when the ballot encourages straight-ticket voting, and their fates are largely defined by party attachment and the strength of top-of-the-ballot candidates. Given that the importance of top-of-the-ballot races trumps down-ballot races, it may be difficult for incumbent mayors to attract voters to the party ticket when the ballot encourages straight-ticket voting. But if voters can easily split their vote – supporting candidates from different tickets/parties for different contests at stake – the candidate's personal reputation has the potential to lure more votes.

Furthermore, the ballot form may motivate candidates to increase their efforts within their district to develop their personal vote, rather than simply focusing on turning out more voters for the party. For instance, in addition to controlling powerful local machines that allow them to turnout-the-vote (Szwarcberg 2013), mayors in Argentina are significant political actors who direct the allocation of government resources and public services (Feierherd and Lucardi 2022; Garay and Maroto 2019; Garay and Simison 2022). They can use these resources to further cultivate a personal vote. We thus posit the incumbency hypothesis.

> *Incumbency Hypothesis.* In down-ballot races, incumbents competing on the electronic ballot will enjoy a larger incumbency bonus, than incumbents competing on the paper ballot.

---

over a decade ago in rural Salta, and because candidates who have held higher positions, such as governors or national legislators, very rarely seek mayor's office.

[21] Table II-4–1 in OA. Models examine the influence of candidate experience on the vote share, between 2007 and 2019, using municipality-level candidate data.

Importantly, many of these factors such as name recognition and experience in office are not exclusive to incumbents. Other officeholders may enjoy similar electoral advantages when competing for an elected position. Current and former legislators are tested campaigners, who are often well known in their districts, and they may count on established political networks to support them. That said, they do not have the same control over resources or visibility derived from holding the mayoral office as incumbent mayors, consequently the overall experience bonus should be smaller than the incumbency bonus. Consistent with this observation, our data shows that former and current provincial legislators performed better than the average mayoral candidate, but only enjoy about half of the bonus of incumbent mayors. We thus evaluate the experience hypothesis.

> *Experience Hypothesis.* In down-ballot races, (current and former) legislators competing for mayor on the electronic ballot will enjoy a larger bonus, than legislators competing for mayor on the paper ballot.

Candidate Gender: An Uneven Playing Field?

Candidate sex is another piece of information voters use to make decisions. Bauer (2020) explains that although people may evaluate individual women candidates as competent when assessing the minimal skills necessary to be a politician, voters evaluate women candidates more negatively than men when forming broad inferences. Consequently, women have to be better qualified to fare as well as their male counterparts. Voters hold women to higher standards than their male competition and are less likely to cast their ballot in favor of women candidates. In line with this observation, scholars frequently find that women come under more scrutiny when running for office (Boussalis et al. 2021; Saxton and Barnes 2022; Teele et al. 2018). Likewise, observational research on U.S. elections that accounts for candidate quality finds that women garner fewer votes at the polls than equally qualified men (Barnes et al. 2017).

Although there is evidence that subtle forms of gender bias influence women's prospects at the polls, it is also possible that voters have overt preferences for male candidates. Setzler (2019) showed, for example, that about 20 percent of survey respondents in 2012 in Argentina agreed or strongly agreed that men make better political leaders than women. This finding is consistent with broader trends from Latin America. Morgan and Buice (2013) find a sizable minority of voters openly agree that men make better political leaders. Importantly, voters are more likely to rely on information-cues such as candidates' sex in low-information settings such as down-ballot races (Anzia and Bernhard 2022; Barnes and Beaulieu 2014; Bernhard and Freeder 2020).

In the case of Salta, we observe that women do not perform as well as men at the polls.[22] Among mayoral candidates competing in municipalities across Salta from 2007 to 2019, our data shows that women candidates underperform the average candidate by 5 percentage points. This finding holds even after controlling for the incumbency of gubernatorial candidates at the top of the ticket and the number of mayoral candidates in the race. The relationship is smaller, however, and not significant when looking at parties with only one mayoral candidate in the district, suggesting that women are relatively better-off in less crowded electoral fields.

We anticipate that if either subtle or obvert gender bias against women is at work in the electorate, then ballots that encourage voters to make discrete decisions for each race at stake will divert support from female candidates competing in down-ballot races. That is, if ballot splitting is made easy, voters who have implicit or explicit preferences against women candidates can effortlessly choose a different mayoral candidate. We thus test the following hypotheses:

> *Women versus Women Hypothesis.* Women will garner a smaller vote share under ballots that facilitate split-ticket voting than under those that discourage it.

> *Women versus Men Hypothesis.* Women will garner a smaller vote share than men, when both are competing under ballots that facilitate split-ticket voting.

Assessing the Influence of Individual Attributes on the Performance of Candidates

Whereas the previous section relied on a matched sample from the Capital Department, the main empirical analysis in this section employs a cross-sectional analysis leveraging municipality-level candidate data from the entire province of Salta over four mayoral elections. The province is divided into 23 departments, which host a total of 60 municipalities. Mayors are elected in every municipality, once every four years, for four-year terms. Every municipality in the sample used a single voting procedure, either paper ballots or electronic voting. We examine 1,185 municipality-level party observations between 2007 and 2019 to assess the ballot effect on the electoral performance of incumbent and women candidates.[23]

To capture the influence of the voting procedure, we estimated a set of linear regression models:

---

[22] Table II-4–2 in OA. Models examine the influence of candidate gender on the vote share, between 2007 and 2019, using municipality-level candidate data.

[23] Differently to the empirical strategy followed in the previous section, which leverages over a quasi-experimental design, this section includes data of all the elections for which there is municipality-level candidate information available.

$$y_{pj} = Perf_{pj} \sim N\left(X_{pj}\beta, \sigma^2\right)$$

Each observation in the data is a municipality-level party observation. The main dependent variable, $Perf_{pj}$, is the electoral performance of a candidate p in municipality j, measured as the difference of her vote share, relative to the gubernatorial candidate at the top of the ticket: values go positive when the mayoral candidate outperformed the gubernatorial one.[24]

The main independent variables in the equation are (a) candidate experience, (b) candidate gender, and (c) ballot type. However, we estimated different equations when examining the influence of experience:

$$X_{pj}\beta = \alpha + \beta_1 eVot_{pj} + \beta_2 incumb_{pj} + \beta_3 legExp_{pj} + \beta_4 eVot_{pj} * incumb_{pj}$$
$$+ \beta_5 eVot_{pj} * legExp_{pj} + \beta Z_{pj}$$

And when examining the influence of gender:

$$X_{pj}\beta = \alpha + \beta_1 eVot_{pj} + \beta_2 gender_{pj} + \beta_3 eVot_{pj} * gender_{pj} + \beta Z_{pj}$$

The ballot effect should be reflected in the corresponding interaction terms. Finally, the Z vector comprises a set of potentially intervening factors.

Gubernatorial candidates may field more than one mayoral candidate in the same municipality. Thus, to calculate the score, the gubernatorial vote share is divided by the number of mayoral candidates. To confirm the reliability of this measure, we also present results for a subset of the sample comprising party tickets with only one mayoral candidate.

Additionally, using the exact same research design as the one employed in Section 3, we examine precinct-level candidate data from the mayoral election in the City of Salta in 2011. This municipality used both voting procedures in that year, allowing us to compare the performance of candidates, in the exact same institutional and party environment, except for the ballot form in place.

The rest of the section examines the ballot effect, first, on incumbent candidates, and second, on female candidates.

The Influence of the Ballot Structure on the Incumbency Advantage

Candidates who ran for office in the past will certainly have advantages over neophytes. Incumbents are candidates who enjoy large name recognition and significant organizational resources, which they will exploit when running for reelection. Current and former provincial legislators are

---

[24] Tables include, for descriptive purposes, models using the candidate's municipality-level vote share, as dependent variable.

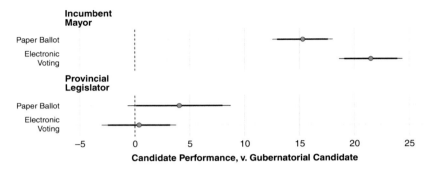

Figure 12 Expected candidate performance, relative to the gubernatorial candidate, by experience and ballot type (90 percent and 95 percent C.I.), based on data from the Province of Salta, 2007–2019

Note: Model predictions based on model 1, in Table II-4–3, in the OA. Omitted variables, held at median values.

officeholders who may exploit similar electoral advantages when running for mayor. Over this period, about one in every four candidates had experience in either position: the province-wide sample comprises 187 incumbents (15.8 percent), as well as 97 candidates with some legislative experience (8.2 percent). A fraction of them, 18 mayoral candidates (1.5 percent), were incumbents with additional experience in the provincial legislature.

Does electronic voting benefit experienced candidates? Figure 12 presents model predictions, showing the expected performance of a mayoral candidate relative to the gubernatorial candidate at the top of the ticket based on their background. When a mayoral candidate gets the same vote share as the gubernatorial candidate, the value is zero (dashed line). When a mayoral candidate outperforms the gubernatorial candidate, values are positive.

Model predictions show that incumbent mayors running in municipalities using electronic devices outperform incumbents competing in municipalities still using paper ballots by 6.2 percentage points. This gap is statistically significant. The same does not hold for candidates with a legislative background. They do not perform significantly better or worse in elections using electronic devices. Moreover, if we compare the performance of provincial legislators against incumbent mayors, the performance gap is substantially wider under electronic devices than under paper ballots: an increase from 11.3 to 21.1 percentage points. Although legislators may be visible political figures, they are not as effective as incumbents at developing a personal brand, and they are not comparably able to exploit the advantages that electronic devices create for personal votes.[25]

---

[25] Table II-4–3 in OA. Models examine the electoral performance of mayoral candidates, relative to the gubernatorial candidate at the top of the ticket.

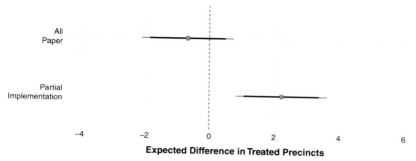

Figure 13 Expected difference in incumbent mayor's performance in treated precincts, relative to control precincts, by implementation stage (90 percent and 95 percent C.I.), based on data from the City of Salta, 2007 and 2011

Note: Model predictions based on model 1, in Table II-4-4, in the OA. Omitted variables, held at median values.

Mayoral elections in the City of Salta provide a robustness check of the incumbency advantage that we observed in the entire sample, now exploiting much more granular data in a quasi-experimental setting.[26] Miguel Isa, the city mayor, ran for reelection in two consecutive turns, 2007 and 2011, and the gubernatorial candidate at the top of the ticket, Governor Urtubey, remained the same in both elections. This municipality used both voting procedures in 2011, allowing us to compare the performance of the same incumbent in the exact same election, except for the voting procedure in place. The previous election, in which all voters used the same ballot form, offers a baseline.

Model results confirm the incumbency advantage observed in the cross-sectional analysis. Figure 13 plots the marginal effect of electronic voting on the incumbency advantage for the 2007 (all paper ballots) and 2011 (partial implementation) elections. In 2007, when all candidates competed on the paper ballot, the incumbency bonus across treatment and control groups was indistinguishable from zero (dashed line). However, in 2011, under partial implementation, the mayoral candidate experienced a significantly larger incumbency advantage in precincts where he competed on an electronic ballot, than in precincts where he competed on a paper ballot: Miguel Isa did about 2.2 percent better in electronic voting precincts, confirming our expectation that personal vote-earning attributes, such as incumbency, matter more in districts with electronic voting than in districts with paper ballots.

---

[26] Table II-4-4 the OA. Models examine precinct-level data of one incumbent mayor running for reelection, in a single municipality in two consecutive renovations. The incumbent mayor did not run for reelection in 2015, hence the full implementation is not included in the analysis.

The results are overall very consistent across the two analyses. Incumbent mayors performed significantly better when voting procedures reduced the costs of making independent choices at the ballot box, allowing them to cultivate a personal connection with their constituencies. The same is not true for candidates with a legislative background; electronic voting made them weaker in comparison to incumbent mayors. Candidates with larger personal resources can exploit the institutional environment created by the new ballot form, concentrating the campaign message around their personal figure, becoming much more independent from the fate of their own party.

The Influence of the Ballot Structure on Women's Opportunities

Unlike incumbents, women are relatively disadvantaged candidates. Evidence often shows that a portion of the electorate has (implicit or explicit) biases against women competing for public office, making them more likely to vote for a man instead of a woman. Over this period, the province-wide sample comprises 172 female mayoral candidates (14.5 percent), and the vast majority of them had no previous office experience, as defined in this section. There were only 11 female incumbents and 16 female legislators in a pool of 1,185 candidates.

Does electronic voting undermine the electoral chances of female candidates? Overall, model results present a relationship in the expected direction, but the results are statistically weak.[27] Figure 14 presents model predictions

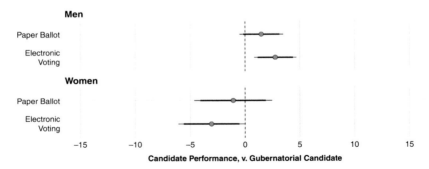

Figure 14 Expected candidate performance, relative to the gubernatorial candidate, by gender and ballot type (90 percent and 95 percent C.I.), based on data from the Province of Salta, 2007–2019

Note: Model predictions based on model 1, in Table II-4–5, in the OA. Omitted variables, held at median values.

---

27 Table II-4–5 in OA. Models examine the effect of ballot forms on the electoral performance of a mayoral candidate, relative to the gubernatorial candidate at the top of the ticket; the second model, replicating the case selection in Table II-4–1, includes tickets with only one mayoral candidate.

showing the expected electoral performance of a mayoral candidate, relative to the gubernatorial candidate at the top of the ticket, based on their gender. Women competing under electronic devices seem to present poorer electoral performances than women competing under partisan paper ballots. A female candidate competing under electronic voting underperforms the gubernatorial candidate by 3.07 points, while an equivalent candidate is expected to underperform by only 1.08 points, but differences between women in each ballot type do not attain conventional levels of statistical difference.

Women do, however, garner a smaller vote share under electronic devices than men competing under the same procedures. The model expects that an average male candidate, holding all other covariates in their means, will over perform the gubernatorial candidate by 2.77 percentage points, while a female candidate will underperform by 3.07 points – a statistically significant 5.8-point gap. That gap when comparing male and female candidates competing in elections using paper ballots is smaller and does not attain conventional levels of statistical significance, suggesting that the new voting procedure puts women candidates in a more difficult environment. However, these results are not consistently strong across all model specifications, raising questions of robustness.

Women running for mayor underperform the average male candidate in Salta elections. While this gender difference might be the result of multiple factors in play, from campaign resources to experience, to the prevalence of misogynistic voters, what is clear is that women's underperformance relative to men's increases with electronic voting. Overall, model results suggest that the use of a ballot form that undermines election coattails may additionally weaken the electoral performances of women competing for down-ballot offices. The evidence, however, is not conclusive, and these hypotheses deserve further examination.

Conclusions

Ballot designs can reinforce the saliency of information about parties and candidates. The design of the ballot can focus voters' attention on the most important races (Rusk 1970; Walker 1966). Party symbols and photographs placed on the ballot provide information commonly used by voters as a heuristic. Whereas party logos are informational cues that may favor parties with higher campaign spending and more recognizable labels (Calvo et al. 2009; Katz et al. 2011), pictures of candidates convey information about age, gender, ethnicity, and physical appearance that favors more attractive candidates (Banducci et al. 2008, Tchintian 2018) and increases ethnic voting by priming identity considerations (Moehler and Conroy-Krutz 2016). Our findings contribute by showing that some ballot forms can reinforce the influence of candidate attributes on voters' decisions.

This section presented evidence of how ballot structures influence individual candidates in down-ballot races. In an environment where ballots diminish straight-ticket voting and party attachments are less influential, candidates will be more likely to depend on their personal attributes and reputation. In the opening example in this section, we suggested that local parties would fare better when coattails are weaker, because they can disassociate their campaign from the top of the ticket, and instead campaign on the personal reputation of their candidates. Consistent with this, we observe that, after the adoption of the electronic devices, personal vote-earning attributes exert a stronger influence on election outcomes. For incumbents, this means they are even further advantaged at the polls. For women, our results suggest that where personal vote-earning attributes are more important, women may face a small penalty, earning slightly fewer votes than their male counterparts. Given the limited variation in the data, further research in a context with more women candidates is needed to understand the extent to which this relationship holds.

Voters derive ideas about candidates' aptitudes from a variety of cues. Our analysis is limited to past political careers and gender. We anticipate that the same type of ballot structure would increase the salience of other personal vote-earning attributes such as race, ethnicity, national or local origin, or even charisma and personality. Future work should explore the propensity of ballot structures to advantage or penalize candidates based on these characteristics and attributes. Down-ballot candidates with enough name recognition may run more personalized campaigns, organized around their own figure, instead of running as part of a larger team. Likewise, local parties like ConVocación por San Isidro, introduced in the opening section, may benefit from ballot forms that diminish coattail effects.

Such ballot forms can reduce the influence of national politics on the election of local officers, making it easier for candidates, parties, and citizens to focus on local issues. Beyond this, either exacerbating or downplaying some candidate features, ballots may have significant implications for democracy overall. Making incumbents more powerful candidates, the ballot form may inadvertently undermine the competitiveness of local elections, creating larger barriers for potential challengers. And, by reinforcing the position of (gender, ethnic, or else) dominant elites, the ballot form may diminish electoral opportunities for historically marginalized groups, making their incorporation to office more difficult. Unintended consequences of ballot reform—such as weakened political parties and less competitive elections—may be particularly detrimental in week or unconsolidated democracies.

5 The Decline of Territorial Machines: The Implications for Parties

Debates over a national ballot reform resurfaced in Argentina in 2022. A coalition of representatives from opposition parties cosponsored a bill intended to replace the partisan paper ballot with a paper Australian ballot in national elections. A chief criticism of the partisan paper ballot is that it places an outsized burden on political parties. Each party competing in national elections is responsible for printing their own ballots, distributing them to all voting centers, and monitoring the ballot supply at polling places on the election day.

Adrián Pérez, former Secretary for Political Affairs (2015–2019) who advocated for ballot reform during his tenure, defended the adoption of an Australian ballot during the 2022 House committee hearings. He maintained that partisan ballots bent the elections in favor of major parties. Reflecting on his earlier efforts to reform the ballot, he recounted previous considerations: "The Electoral Court ... said there is a need to guarantee each individual voter's right, so that she can vote for the party that she selected before arriving at the ballot box. And, for multiple different reasons, a partisan ballot does not guarantee this right: due to ballot stealing, due to the absence of party monitors, due to the post office not delivering the ballots in time, due to whatever reason. But certainly, voters in many cases could not vote for their preferred option."[28]

During the same series of House hearings, Alejandro Tullio, former National Electoral Director (2001–2015), argued the burden the ballot design imposes on parties is unevenly distributed. "The uniformity of the electoral offer across the national geography is dependent on the economic and logistical ability of the political parties. It is true that [in national elections] the Post Office ... makes a first provision, to the extent that the Electoral Court tells it, of a certain number of ballots for all the polling stations. ... But that is not enough. ... We are not only talking about printing costs, but also incremental logistical costs ... fundamentally for parties. And the costs are not only budgetary, they are organizational costs, they are energies that parties must put into that, instead of campaigning and making their proposals known to the citizens."[29]

---

[28] Original quote: "La Cámara Nacional Electoral ... decía [que] hay que garantizar el derecho a cada elector de que pueda votar la oferta electoral que había elegido previamente a entrar al cuarto oscuro. Y esto con un sistema de boleta partidaria no estaba garantizado por distintas razones: por un problema de robo de boleta, porque faltaban fiscales, porque el correo en algún lugar no llegó con la distribución, por lo que fuera. Pero ciertamente [los] electores, en muchos casos, no podían votar la opción elegida." https://youtu.be/Tt7nkFjmKaw?t=1497, accessed on May 26, 2022.

[29] Original quote: "La universalidad de la oferta electoral en toda la geografía nacional está condicionada por la capacidad económica y logística de los partidos políticos. Es cierto que el Correo ... hace una primera distribución, en la medida que la Justicia le dice, [de] una

By contrast, the Australian ballot ensures that all the options are available at the ballot box. Tullio explained the Australian ballot "guarantees the voters that they will be able to choose whoever they want regardless of the logistical capacity of the party and guarantees the parties a greater fairness in the competition."[30]

This certainly rings true for the ballot reform in Salta. Parties with fewer resources and weaker logistical capacity were disproportionately disadvantaged when competing on partisan paper ballots. But, as we illustrate, the adoption of the electronic ballot changed the game. In this section, we turn to parties, arguing that ballot designs also impose various coordination and campaign costs on political parties. These additional costs ultimately inform the electoral geography of parties – that is, *where* they can garner votes and how their votes are distributed across the district.

The Influence of Ballots on Campaign Strategies

The geographical distribution of electoral constituencies can shape outcomes and party strategies. Asymmetrical geographical distributions of preferences are associated with electoral biases. Democrats in the United States (Rodden 2010) and Laborists in the United Kingdom (Calvo and Rodden 2015), for example, are concentrated in cities. Larger majoritarian biases in election rules penalize their chances of electing representatives. This is not necessarily the effect of gerrymandered districts, but the geographical distribution of voters. As Gudgin and Taylor (1976: 14, emphasis in the original) summarized it, "*any* division of an electorate into constituencies will have *some* political effect by the very nature of the problem." Importantly, biases in the translation of votes into seats are likely replicated in the transformation of preferences into policies.

Geography can also shape party strategies and campaigns. There is a geography of campaign contributions. Donor support bases in the United States are often clustered in highly educated, wealthy urban areas (Gimpel et al. 2006), but their campaign contributions are often directed to races in competitive districts that might be hundreds or even thousands of miles away

---

determinada cantidad de boletas para todas las mesas electorales. . . . Pero eso no alcanza. . . . No solamente estamos hablando de costos de impresión, sino de costos logísticos incrementales . . . fundamentalmente para los partidos políticos. Y los costos no son sólo financieros, son costos de organización, son energías que deben ponerse en eso, en lugar de hacer campaña y hacer conocer las propuestas a los ciudadanos." https://youtu.be/ZlBQ-9hvmo0?t=10637, accessed on May 26, 2022.

[30] Original quote: "La boleta única papel (BUP) asegura la integridad de la oferta electoral. . . . Garantiza a los electores que van a poder escoger a quien deseen sin importar la capacidad logística de la agrupación, y a las agrupaciones una mayor equidad en la competencia". https://cenital.com/boleta-unica-ventajas-desventajas-y-las-reformas-adicionales/, accessed on May 26, 2022.

(Gimpel et al. 2008). There are also geographic constraints underlying parties' electoral performance. Leveraging a set of European democracies, Potter and Olivella (2015) present evidence that parties are more likely to enter districts that are closer to other ones where the party has fielded candidates. Harbers (2017), examining Mexican elections, shows that party support in one district increases the likelihood of party support nearby. And, more importantly for our purpose, geography shapes electioneering too. Party campaigns target neighborhoods where strategists believe that party supporters are concentrated (Carty and Eagles 1999).

Parties and candidates have limited resources to campaign, thus developing an effective mobilization strategy is a fundamental challenge for any party organization. Candidates have limited time to spend knocking on voters' doors and canvassing. Parties have limited cash to print street banners and posters or to buy ads in the local media to advertise their names across the district territory. Party volunteers might provide some organizational means, for example, lending places to set up campaign offices. Regardless, parties need to devote large campaign efforts to establish a party network over an extended territory. Latner and McGann (2005) present evidence from Israel and the Netherlands that, even in highly proportional institutional settings, party competition may develop within-district regional patterns, despite that an extra vote counts the same wherever it is won. Alles, Pachón and Muñoz (2021), leveraging data from three decades of Colombian elections, show that such strategic considerations are driven by voting procedures. Effective party campaigns need to make careful decisions when allocating resources.

The printing and distribution of election ballots is one such campaign effort. First, party organizations must bear the expense of printing paper ballots, consuming resources that could otherwise be used to cover the costs of campaign activities. Second, party organizations need to distribute the ballots to polling places across the department, sometimes located in polling places many miles apart. Third, parties need to make ballots available to the voters on election day; this requires parties to monitor polling places to ensure that they do not run out of ballots and that rivals do not steal or sabotage their ballots. The first issue imposes a budgetary burden on parties. Solving the latter two issues demand a well-established party machine to provide an on-the-ground presence during elections.

Parties and candidates face strong incentives to concentrate campaign efforts in the most efficient manner. Campaigning everywhere could be a wasted effort if parties cannot assure that the ballots will be available at every voting center. In a situation like this, parties may opt to concentrate their campaign efforts on key locations, where they can rely on local networks to distribute ballots and monitor polling places, rather than spreading them across the entire district.

The adoption of electronic voting transfers most of these costs to the electoral authority or eliminates them entirely. First, electronic voting eliminates the financial cost associated with the printing and distribution of ballots. Second, the electoral authority is entirely responsible for the allocation of devices in every polling place, ensuring that all parties and candidates are available options at the ballot box. And finally, the risk of sabotage is minimal: there is no equivalent of stealing the other party's ballots when an electronic device is in place. As the adoption of electronic voting effectively transfers the burden of ballot provision to the electoral authority and significantly reduces the costs associated with monitoring voting centers, campaign efforts are less constrained by the geographical scope of party machines. So, parties can expand their campaigns to areas previously dominated by other factions or parties, resulting in a larger dispersion of the electoral support. Consequently, we expect to observe support for the following hypothesis:

> *Logistics Hypothesis.* Parties competing under electronic devices will present a more geographically dispersed electoral base.

Measuring Vote Concentration in Legislative Elections

We employ a cross-sectional analysis leveraging department-party level data to examine the effect of ballot type on the geographical concentration of party votes. We examine 552 party lists competing for province House seats and 392 party lists competing for province Senate seats, distributed over six election cycles from 2009 to 2019. Parties in the sample ran in districts using paper ballots in the first two cycles – that is, 2009 and 2011; and using electronic devices since the 2013 renovation. As we detailed in Section 2, races in four departments (i.e., Capital, La Caldera, Metán, Orán) used both voting procedures simultaneously in 2011: they are thus excluded from the sample to provide a clear contrast between treatments.

To capture the influence of the voting procedure, we estimated a set of Beta regression models. The dependent variable can only assume values in the unit interval: $Gini_{pk}$ goes from 0 to 1 and a Beta distribution accommodates a variable of such characteristics (Cribari-Neto and Zeileis 2010; Ferrari and Cribari-Neto 2004).

$$y_{pk} = Gini_{pk} \sim Beta\left(\mu_{pk}, \varphi\right)$$

Each observation in the data is a department-party level observation. The term $Gini_i$ captures the vote concentration of party p in department k; it is distributed over a beta density with mean μ_{pk} and precision φ. The term $g(.)$ is a strictly monotonic link function, which may adopt multiple forms – models were estimated using a logit link.

$$\mu_{pk} = g\left(\eta_{pk}\right) = logit^{-1}\left(\eta_{pk}\right)$$

$$\eta_{pk} = X_{ij}\beta + \varepsilon_{ij}$$

$$X_{ij}\beta = \alpha + \beta_1 eVot_{ij} + \beta_2 votes_{ij} + \beta_3 votes_{ij}^2 + \beta_4 eVot_{ij} * votes_{ij} + \beta Z_{ij}$$

The term η_{pk} is a linear predictor introducing a set of explanatory variables in the statistical model: β are a set of regression coefficients capturing the effect of some X vector of independent party-level variables on $Gini_{pk}$, the Z vector comprises a set of potentially intervening factors, and ε_{pk} is an error term. The parameter φ is a precision parameter: it is left constant in the model estimation.

The dependent variable, $Gini_{pk}$, is a measure of the geographical concentration of party votes, which following previous research (Alles et al. 2021; Bochsler 2010; Calvo and Rodden 2015), is captured by a Gini Index. We calculated the Gini Index for each party list p, in the kth department, in the tth election cycle.[31] The index equals 0 when the distribution of partisan votes across a department's ballot boxes mirrors the exact geographical distribution of valid votes. The measure approaches 1 when all the votes of a given party are concentrated in a single voting booth. The median value in the sample is 0.282, and three-fourth of the observations fall in a score range between 0.112 and 0.533.[32]

The X vector comprises a set of independent and control variables. The main independent variable in the models is the type of ballot: elections using electronic voting are coded 1, and 0 when using paper ballots. The most important control in the equation is the vote percentage: larger parties tend to show a more even geographical distribution. Most of the election rules other than the ballot form remained constant all over the period; district magnitude, which varies by department only in House elections, is a covariate in the equation. The models control for potentially intervening institutional and sociodemographic factors – that is,

---

[31] The Gini Index compares the distribution of vote shares across ballot boxes, and it is calculated based on about 223,500 booth-level party observations, over six election cycles, between 2009 and 2019.

[32] Alternatively, the G-Index is a department-party level measure of vote concentration (Peres da Silva and Davidian 2013; Avelino et al. 2016); empirical results using the G-Index instead of Gini are consistent with those reported for the main models.

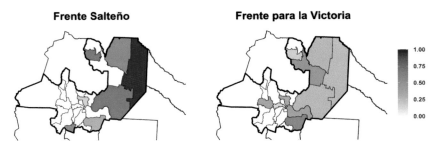

Figure 15 Vote concentration of two (selected) parties, competing in provincial House elections in Salta: Frente para la Victoria and Frente Salteño (Province of Salta, 2009)
Source: Tile map by INDEC <www.indec.gob.ar/indec/web/Institucional-Indec-Codgeo>

population density, area, number of voting booths, urbanization, educational attainment, and poverty.

The Geographical Implications of Ballot Reform

The geographical concentration of party votes may vary considerably across departments. The same party may garner an uneven distribution of votes in some departments (i.e., preforming well in some precincts and near absent in others), while garnering a more even or homogeneous distribution of votes in other places. Although a portion of that variation is associated with the party performance, given that small parties tend to show more concentrated vote patterns, ballot forms that hand the ballot provision over parties exacerbate this type of difference. Figure 15 illustrates these regional contrasts for two parties with similar overall performances in 2009, two years before the reform implementation, when every polling place in the province used paper ballots.

The left panel presents the department-level vote concentration of the Frente Salteño, a party that ran in 7 departments, winning three House seats and combining 11.8 percent of province votes. Party votes were fairly dispersed in the Capital Department, and to a lesser degree, in Rosario de la Frontera Department: the party's Gini Index was 0.115 and 0.288, respectively. However, in other departments, the party performance was heavily concentrated in a limited number of places. The party's Gini Index in Anta Department, where the party attracted a respectable 12.2 percent of the votes, was an outstanding 0.668; and the score was above 0.500 in all the remaining departments. By contrast, the right-hand presents a party with a very similar overall performance, but much more homogeneous vote distributions. The Frente para la Victoria (Peronist Party) ran in 10 departments, and it got four House seats thanks to 10.2 percent of province votes. Party votes were fairly

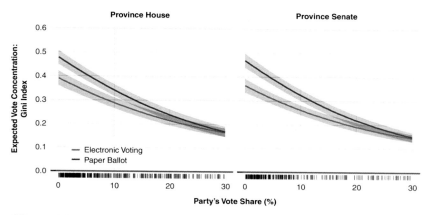

Figure 16 Expected gini index in provincial House and Senate elections, by ballot type and electoral support (95 percent C.I.), based on data from the Province of Salta, 2009–2019

Note: Model predictions based on models 2 and 4, in Table II-5–1, in the OA. Omitted variables, held at median values.

dispersed in Chicoana and Iruya departments, with concentration scores below 0.150. The score only rose above 0.500 in one department, Rosario de la Frontera.

Evidence from our analysis shows that the ballot form is strongly linked to the geographical concentration of votes. Higher concentrations are more likely when parties need to print and distribute their own ballots.[33] Legislative elections under paper ballots presented higher levels of geographical concentration of votes compared to elections using electronic devices. This effect is, nevertheless, conditional on the party size: geographical concentration is, regardless of the voting procedure, roughly the same among parties garnering 20 percent of the votes or more, whereas the use of electronic voting makes a substantive difference for small parties.

Figure 16 reports the expected level of geographical concentration of votes for different ballot forms and different parties' vote shares, holding other variables at their median values. First, factions competing in elections using electronic devices consistently attracted votes in a more even distribution throughout the department. The Gini Index is expected to fall from 0.406 to 0.336 for a party competing in House elections that gets 5 percent of the votes; this difference is statistically significant. Additionally, when comparing House and Senate races, the model results are very consistent. The concentration is

---

[33] Table II-5–1 in OA. Models examine two samples: province House and province Senate elections.

expected to fall from 0.392 to 0.309, for a senatorial candidate who gets the same share of votes.

Second, parties with large electoral support most often have a geographically extended base and are thus expected to present a lower Gini score. Yet, the ballot form mediates this relationship: concentration differences between large and small parties were larger under paper ballots. The expected geographical concentration falls from 0.406 to 0.239 (i.e., −0.167) when a party competing in House elections moves from 5 percent to 20 percent of the votes before the reform. Very similar changes are expected for senatorial races (from 0.392 to 0.220). After the adoption of electronic voting, the difference in vote concentration between parties of different sizes declined considerably. In such cases, the index score falls from 0.336 to 0.215 (i.e., −0.121), when comparing a party of 5 percent to another one of 20 percent of the votes. In sum, the use of electronic voting is heavily affecting the geographical distribution of support of small parties. For parties that garner about 20 percent of the votes, procedures do not make a meaningful difference.

Similar effects were observed after the adoption of an Australian ballot in Colombia (see Alles et al. 2021), though the magnitude of the transformation was smaller in the case of Salta. Before the Colombian ballot reform, the electoral support of party factions presented significantly higher levels of geographical concentration than their peers in Salta, thus the space for change was larger as well. Nevertheless, the overall pattern between the outcomes of both reforms is considerably similar. Decreasing the logistic burden of the election is associated with more even distributions of votes, and such changes are larger among small parties.

The QQ plot displayed in Figure 17 illustrates the substantive implications of changes in the vote concentration, by representing how party votes deviate from a uniform vote distribution. The x-axis plots the theoretical quantile values of the standard normal distribution. The y-axis plots the corresponding quantile values of the party votes in the actual data. A straight horizontal line would represent a party that is getting the same vote share in every voting booth – that is, a concentration index of 0. A straight diagonal instead would represent a party with a normally distributed vote concentration. Each panel compares the distribution of votes by ballot box for two pairs of parties competing in House elections: a party competing under paper ballots in blue and a party competing under electronic devices in red. The parties represented in the figures were selected because they fall almost exactly in the model predictions, offering a clear picture of the ballot effect on comparable parties.

The left-hand panel of Figure 17 presents the vote distribution for two small parties competing in districts with the same magnitude (three seats) and the

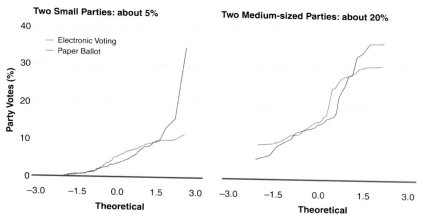

Figure 17 Distribution of votes of four (selected) parties, competing in provincial House elections, by voting procedure and party size

Note: The left-hand panel presents the distribution of votes of Salta Somos Todos, in the Anta Department in 2009 (in blue); and of Partido Obrero, in the Metán Department in 2013 (red). The right-hand panel presents the distribution of votes of Partido de la Victoria, in the Santa Victoria Department in 2011 (blue); and of Partido Justicialista, in La Caldera Department in 2015 (red).

same number of competitors (nine). We chose to feature these two parties as examples because their electoral fortunes closely align with our model predictions of how the vote concentration will vary depending on the ballot type. This makes them great illustrations of how two alternative distributions of votes look. Salta Somos Todos (blue line), in Anta Department in 2009, competed under a paper ballot and its electoral fortunes best represent the model baseline for the control group: a geographical concentration index score (the DV) of 0.413, getting roughly 4.73 percent of votes. The vote distribution is highly skewed, with a large share of its votes coming from a small number of ballot boxes. This relationship is apparent at the right end of the plot, where the line becomes almost vertical. This narrow concentration of votes is expected for small parties using the partisan paper ballot because small parties like Salta Somos Todos cannot afford to distribute ballots to all of the voting booths in the district.

Contrast this with a similar party, the Partido Obrero (red line), in the Metán Department that used an electronic ballot in 2013. The Partido Obrero had a geographical concentration index score of 0.342 and attained 5.27 percent of votes. The distribution of votes for Partido Obrero more closely approximates a normal distribution, indicating that their vote shares were more evenly distributed across voting booths. Just like Salta Somos Todos, Partido Obrero cannot afford to distribute ballots across all of the voting centers in their district. But, when using electronic devices, they do not have to. Instead, the Partido Obrero automatically appears on every ballot box. As a result, they can garner votes in each voting center across the entire district.

The right-hand panel presents two medium-sized parties competing in districts with the same magnitude (one seat) and the same number of competing parties (five). In this case, both parties are large enough to have the necessary resources to print and provide ballots across the entire district. For this reason, their distribution of votes should not be significantly different when using different ballot types. In Figure 17 we observe that the differences between vote distributions for the party using electronic ballots compared to the party using the partisan paper ballot were significantly smaller than the differences observed in the case of small parties.

Partido de la Victoria (blue line), in the Santa Victoria Department, used paper ballots in 2011, and represents the model baseline in this case. An index score of 0.250 is fairly close to the model expectation for a party getting 18.00 percent of the votes. Notably, this distribution is very similar to the model prediction for similar-sized parties using the electronic ballot. Consider next the Partido Justicialista (red line), in La Caldera Department, which used the electronic ballot in 2015. It provides an ideal case for illustrating the treatment effect for medium parties. An index score of 0.217 is about the expectation for 18.41 percent of the votes. In both cases, the distribution of votes closely approximates the normal, regardless of the ballot type. Whereas the distribution of votes for small parties is sensitive to the logistics of the provision of ballots, larger parties with ample resources are less so.

Conclusions

Geography constrains the electoral performance of parties. Parties are more likely to field candidates in districts near other districts where the party is already competing (Potter and Olivella 2015), and their support in one district is linked to their support in nearby districts (Harbers 2017). Candidates and parties face powerful incentives to carefully consider where campaign efforts will be deployed. Although major parties often have resources and networks to organize large campaigns, even large parties benefit from targeting areas where supporters are concentrated (Carty and Eagles 1999). The influence of geography on party strategies and campaigns is, however, mediated by electoral institutions, and in particular, ballots can reinforce or weaken such incentives (Alles et al. 2021).

The results in this section provide further evidence of how the ballot structure shapes the geographical distribution of votes. Experienced electoral officers, as mentioned in the section introduction, indicate that the logistics of the partisan paper ballots create an uneven electoral field, disproportionately harming small parties. The printing and distribution of ballots constrain the campaign strategies of parties, which face incentives to concentrate electioneering efforts in territories where they can call on local networks. After the adoption of electronic devices, the options that voters find at the ballot box are no longer conditional on party resources. Instead, candidates can count on their name being on the ballot across the entire districts. District-wide access to the ballot levels the field for small parties, and this might be especially true when districts encompass large territories, such as an entire province. Some parties may still choose to focus their campaign resources on their traditional fiefdoms where they can rely on established local networks to turn out the votes. Others may play a different game, expanding their campaigns to new territories, resulting in a more even distribution of votes.

Beyond electoral implications, these changes may also influence legislative behavior. Electoral competition exerts pressures on representatives to represent their constituents (Mayhew 1974), but parties and legislators elected by a narrow geographic portion of the district will likely represent a relatively slim set of policy preferences. This is because they do not need to care for the entire district, but only for the bailiwick where their electorate is concentrated. A new ballot form, even under the exact same electoral institutions, can transform the representative connection between legislators and voters, from one where officials are focused on small constituencies, to one where they are attentive to more overarching interests and preferences across the district.

6 The Consequences of Weakened Gubernatorial Coattails: The Implications for Small Parties

Despite relatively high district magnitudes, small parties campaigning in provincial elections across Argentina sometimes struggle to gain a foothold in legislative elections. It is particularly difficult for parties without strong gubernatorial candidates to attract votes to the legislative list. Major parties tend to dominate legislative elections in years where there is a gubernatorial race on the ballot. But, in 2015, the Partido Obrero secured a legislative seat in the Capital District – an unusual victory for the Partido Obrero during a gubernatorial election year.

To vote for a small party in the legislative election, voters must either cast a vote for a non-viable gubernatorial candidate or sink the cost of splitting their ballot. In Argentina, where partisan paper ballots are pervasive, this is an uphill battle for small parties. In stark contrast to the partisan paper ballots, we showed in Section 3 that the new electronic ballot used all across Salta in 2015 reduced the cost of split-ticket voting, making it easier to vote for different parties in different races. Parties in Salta recognized this potential advantage right away. Interviews conducted immediately after the partial implementation in 2011 indicated that campaigners recognized that the new electronic ballot facilitates split-ticket voting (Pomares et al. 2011).

As suggested above, some parties may be better situated than others to capitalize on this reform. Some parties may even be hurt by the reform. In this section, we examine whether some parties are systematically advantaged (or disadvantaged) by the new ballot structure.

Ballot Form and Electoral Coordination

Ballot features influence electoral outcomes, however, this effect could be uneven across parties. Some features may benefit some parties or candidates to the detriment of others (Calvo et al. 2009). Information cues, such as party logos, candidate photos, or organization of the ballot, inform voters' decisions (Tchintian 2018). For instance, party-centric shortcuts favor parties with bigger treasure chests and more recognizable labels and candidates (Katz et al. 2011). Some ballot structures may cause confusion for voters, inducing more frequent voting mistakes among particular groups of voters – ultimately hurting some parties more than others (Tomz and Van Houweling 2003). We likewise anticipate that ballots that facilitate split-ticket voting will benefit some parties more than others.

Strategic voting theory offers insight into which candidates or parties will see the largest uptick resulting from an increase in vote-splitting due to the ballot structure. Cox (1997) argues that voters refrain from voting for their most preferred candidate when they are unlikely to be elected, voting instead for their most preferred viable candidate to avoid wasting their vote. In concurrent elections, multiple candidates vying for different positions compete under the same party label, but each race is often governed by a different set of electoral rules. Whereas a party may not have a viable candidate competing in the executive race owing to the nature of the single member district, candidates competing under the same party label may be competitive in the legislative election where multiple candidates win a seat in office in the same district. Consequently, voters may be compelled to cast a strategic vote in the executive election – supporting a viable candidate – and a sincere vote in the legislative election where their preferred party has a better chance at securing a seat.

The likelihood that a voter will split their ballot to cast a strategic vote in the executive election and a sincere vote in the legislative election is shaped by both, the likelihood that their vote makes a difference and the effort required to split the vote. If the cost of ballot splitting is high – for example, if they have to manually cut the ballot–voters may be less likely to split their ballot if they are uncertain it will make a difference. But, when ballot splitting is costless – as with the electronic ballot – voters may be willing to split their ballot, even if the payoff is unclear.

> *Coordination Hypothesis.* The use of the electronic ballot will lead to fewer votes for candidates competing under the same party label with viable gubernatorial candidates, and more votes for candidates from smaller parties.

Estimating the Impact of the Ballot on Electoral Coordination

Building on the empirical strategy used in Section 3, we return to our quasi-experimental design from the incremental implementation of the electronic ballot across three election periods. Here too, we leverage data from the Capital Department and rely on the Coarsened Exact matched sample introduced in Section 3. The results are consistent regardless of the matching threshold. In this analysis we use party-level data, thus our sample comprises a total of 23 parties competing across 54 precincts, throughout three election cycles.

Each observation in the data is a precinct-level party observation from the matched sample. Given that different parties compete in each election, we cannot use a party-level DiD approach to examine the relationship between ballot form and strategic voting. Instead, we estimated linear models for each election year.

$$y_{pi} = House_{pi} \sim N\left(X_{pi}\beta, \sigma^2\right)$$

$$X_{it}\beta = \alpha + \beta_T T_i + \beta_p Party_{pi} + \beta_{Tp} Party_{pi} * T_i$$

The term $House_{pi}$ captures the strength of the legislative ticket of a party. The term T is a dummy variable that captures possible differences between the treatment and control groups in a given year: $T = 1$ for the treated group. Each running party, captured by a dummy variable, is interacted with by the treatment condition.[34]

---

[34] The dependent variable, $House_{pi}$, is a measure of the relative performance of the legislative ticket in comparison to the gubernatorial candidate of a given party, scaled over the precinct valid votes.

The dependent variable, $House_{pi}$, is a measure of the relative performance of the legislative ticket in comparison to the gubernatorial candidate, calculated for each party list p, in the 0th precinct, in the tth election cycle – the score is positive when the legislative ticket outperformed the gubernatorial candidate. Although the possible values of the variable go from -100 to 100, the observed values in the matched sample go from -13.2 to 10.0, and the median value in the matched sample is 0.08.

The Influence of the Ballot Structure on Electoral Coordination

The provincial Chamber of Deputies (or lower House) is a 60-member body, elected in department-wide districts of different magnitudes. The Capital Department, the largest electoral district, is represented by 19 legislators in the Salta House. Deputies serve for four years and are elected using partial renovation. Every four years nine deputies are elected concurrent with the gubernatorial election. The remaining 10 deputies (and the department's senator) are elected in the midterm cycle. Due to its relatively large magnitude, elections in the district have been significantly fragmented – parties rarely get more than 25 percent of the votes. However, the major gubernatorial candidates are often joined by multiple legislative tickets, reflecting the party composition of their electoral fronts.

The 2007 election was the most competitive gubernatorial race in the sample. The three-term incumbent governor, Juan Carlos Romero, was term-limited. Two candidates emerged as the most prominent competitors to succeed him, each of them representing different factions of the Peronist Party: Walter Wayar and Juan Manuel Urtubey. The gubernatorial election resulted in a very tight race. Urtubey prevailed by about six thousand votes, only 1.2 percent of the province votes.

The competitive environment created strong pressures for electoral coordination among voters. Looking at the election results in the Capital Department, such incentives were clearly at work. Both Wayar (PJ) and Urtubey (FPV-PRS) performed significantly better than their legislative ticket, by 5.7 and 8.7 points, respectively. Many voters voted strategically, defecting from a non-viable gubernatorial candidate, but still supporting their most preferred legislative ticket.[35]

$$House_{pi} = \frac{\left(D_{pi} - G_{pi}\right)}{\sum_{p=1}^{n} G_{pi}} * 100$$

We calculated the score for each party list p, in the ith precinct, in the tth election cycle. The score is positive when the legislative ticket outperformed the gubernatorial candidate: when $House_{pi} = 1$, the slate of representative candidates garnered 1 percentage point (of the overall valid votes) more than the gubernatorial candidate.

[35] Table II-6–1 in the OA.

It appears that voters supporting three minor parties engaged in strategic voting. The legislative ticket of Partido Obrero, Propuesta Salteña, and Concertación Salteña all outperformed the gubernatorial ticket by 0.6 percent to 1.8 percent. As expected, voters in treatment and control groups did not differ in the 2007 election, when all the precincts used the same voting procedures.

The remaining two elections were much less competitive, hence the pressures for electoral coordination were much weaker. Governor Urtubey ran for reelection in 2011. He competed against Alfredo Olmedo, a first-term House representative, with experience as a provincial senator representing the Anta Department; and Walter Wayar, who had been elected House representative in the midterm election cycle. Unlike the previous election, this time Urtubey won by a landslide: he obtained 59.6 percent of the province votes. Olmedo ended in a distant second place, with 25.1 percent. Wayar finished in third place, with 8.5 percent.[36]

Election results in the Capital Department show that Urtubey (FREJUREVI) and Wayar outpreformed their legislative tickets by 4.5 and 4.0 points, respectively. To a lesser degree, a small party candidate, Carlos Morello, outpreformed his party as well. By contrast, despite being the strongest challenger in the race, Olmedo significantly underperformed his legislative ticket by 5.2 points. Voters from the Partido Obrero and Unión Cívica Radical seem to have strategically defected from their gubernatorial candidates as well, though results are weaker. Only the two smallest parties in the race (MIJD and CC-ARI), both winning less than 1 percent of the department vote share, did not see an uptick in split tickets. Given that neither party had a realistic chance of winning a seat in the legislative or gubernatorial election, it is unlikely that their supporters were attempting to cast strategic votes.

Our expectation, building on the strategic voting theory, was that the top gubernatorial candidates in the race would attract more votes than their legislative ticket and that this effect should be significantly more pronounced in precincts using electronic devices. Interestingly, some voters (namely supporters of Olmedo and Wayar) exploit the opportunities created by the electronic ballot and split their tickets significantly more often than voters in precincts using paper ballots. There was a statistically significant increase in the share of split tickets for both candidates in precincts using electronic voting, and the size of the effect was substantial.

Still, the data do not show as clear of a pattern as anticipated. Figure 18 presents the expected margin of the legislative ticket in comparison to the

---

[36] Pollsters anticipated a comfortable advantage of Urtubey over his closest competitors. The polls were reported in *Infobae*, "Salta: las últimas encuestas otorgaban una cómoda victoria para Urtubey," April 10, 2011. www.infobae.com/c574779 (accessed May 7, 2016).

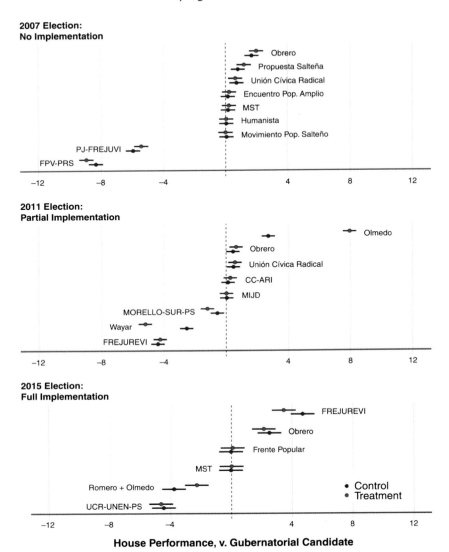

Figure 18 Expected House-Gubernatorial vote margin, by party, implementation stage and treatment group (84 percent C.I.), based on data from the Capital Department, 2007–2015

Note: Model predictions based on models 2, 4, and 6, in Table II-6–1, in the OA. Omitted variables, held at median values.

gubernatorial candidate. The top gubernatorial candidates were not particularly favored by electronic voting. Urtubey (FREJUREVI) did not perform differently with electronic voting or the partisan paper ballot. Meanwhile, Olmedo won fewer votes than did his tandem legislative lists, and this difference was even larger in precincts using electronic devices. Olmedo underperformed his legislative candidates by about 2.7 percentage points among precincts using paper ballots and 8.0 percentage points in precincts with electronic voting.

The gubernatorial candidates from smaller parties were not particularly disadvantaged by electronic voting. Instead, Wayar out preformed his legislative list, and the margin was larger in precincts using electronic devices. Wayar won 2.5 percentage points more votes than his party's legislative list in precincts using paper ballots, and 5.2 points more in precincts using electronic devices. Governors from the remaining four small parties were not more or less advantaged in precincts with the electronic device.

Nevertheless, the results suggest that when split-ticket voting is made easy, smaller parties may do well to develop independent campaign strategies for each office at stake. In this scenario, smaller parties can (more or less overtly) encourage their supporters to split their ticket to support only the party's most viable candidate, in an attempt to avoid loosing supporters who do not want to waste a vote. This is reflected in how the vote-splitting pattern observed in precincts using paper ballots was exacerbated in electronic voting ones. Overall, the gubernatorial candidates who did better than the legislative ticket in precincts with paper ballots, overperformed by even larger margins in precincts with electronic ballots, and vice versa.

The results may also be influenced by the fact that the 2019 election was not very competitive. Governor Urtubey ran for a third and last term in 2015, competing against the then-senator and former three-term governor Juan Carlos Romero, joining forces with the former gubernatorial candidate Alfredo Olmedo as his running-mate. Although the election was closer than four years before, Urtubey defeated Romero by a sizable margin, 47.2 percent versus 33.7 percent. Partido Obrero finished in a distant third place with 7.3 percent of the province votes.

Election results in the Capital Department show that Romero and Miguel Nanni (UCR-UNEN-PS) performed significantly better than their legislative ticket, by 3.0 and 4.5 points, respectively. By contrast, despite being the incumbent governor and front-runner in the race, this time Urtubey significantly underperformed the legislative ticket, by an average of 4.1 points. Voters of Partido Obrero had the same pattern of strategically defecting from their gubernatorial candidate: the slate of legislative candidates bested Claudio del Plá by an average of 2.3 points. Similar to the model results from the first election in the data, there were no statistically significant differences between treatment and control groups in the 2015 election, when all the voters used the same voting procedure. Analyses of the 2007 and 2015 elections indicate that the party differences observed in 2011 were not a product of underlying idiosyncratic conditions between groups but evidence of the effects of the ballot form.

Overall, evidence indicates that parties can exploit the opportunities created by voting procedures to garner more votes for their party. The Wayar and Olmedo examples suggest the effect size is substantial (between 3 to 5 percent of votes).

Are the effects of the ballot form on vote splitting large enough to have electoral implications? To answer this question we consider the district characteristics of the Capital Department in Salta. Parties need about 6.3 percent of the votes to win a seat in the Capital Department where the district magnitude is nine. An extra half a percentage point increases the chance of winning a seat by about 40 percent.[37] Thus, encouraging split-ticket voting in an effort to garner more seats for the legislative ticket, is clearly a viable strategy in this setting.

The performance of Partido Obrero, dicussed in the introduction of this section, illustrates this point. Election after election, the party's legislative ticket attracted more votes than the gubernatorial candidate in the Capital Department – on average, the legislative ticket garnered 1.3 percentage points more. The voting device increased the gap by another half percentage point, and in 2015, when the entire district used the electronic ballot, the Partido Obrero managed to win a seat. One seat is not trivial. There are only nine seats up for grabs in the district. All the remaining House districts have magnitudes from one to three seats, making the Capital Department the only place where a small party may obtain legislative representation.

Conclusions

The evidence offered in this section provides some insights into how parties are differentially affected by changes in the ballot structure. Although there were not observable voting differences for every party, in some cases the ballot form was associated with 3- to 5-point gaps, indicating that the opportunities for legislative parties to run campaigns relatively independent from the gubernatorial election grew considerably thanks to the adoption of electronic voting. The ballot reform created new opportunities for small parties.

The Partido Obrero illustrates how the shift away from partisan paper ballots may have important electoral implications in settings where the effective vote threshold to win a seat is low. In Argentina, for example, multiple provinces with high district magnitudes, which decreases the effective threshold, have piloted electronic devices or introduced paper Australian ballots. Our findings

---

[37] Appendix III presents the results of a simulation of the threshold that parties need to reach to get a first seat, in an election of the characteristics of the one examined in this section: a district magnitude of 9 seats, with a 5 percent formal vote threshold, and using the D'Hondt formula to allocate seats.

indicate that these ballot reforms may manufacture opportunities for small parties to win seats by facilitating ballot splitting.

However, as we can only examine the partial implementation of the ballot reform for one legislative election, we are limited in our ability to offer more generalizable conclusions. Future research should further consider the differential effects of ballot reforms across different political parties, with an eye towards competitive elections, where the incentives for electoral coordination are high.

7 Conclusions

Ballot designs have critical implications for representation. Controversies around voting procedures in the United States in recent decades have commanded considerable attention from scholars, media, and politicians (Beaulieu 2014, 2016; Engstrom and Roberts 2020). Yet, we know far less about the consequences of ballot reforms outside the United States. In this Element, we provided one of the first comprehensive studies of the consequences of ballot structures for representation, examining their influence on the three main actors in elections: voters, candidates, and parties.

This final section summarizes the contributions of our findings to the literature on electoral institutions in particular, and to the research on political representation overall. First, we discuss how the ballot form has the power to transform campaigns and election outcomes. Second, we explain the consequences of the ballot form for policy representation. Finally, we consider the prospects for ballot reform in Argentina more broadly.

Redefining the Electoral Competition

Voting demands time and effort. The ballot form structures the costs voters incur when making choices at the ballot box. Some ballot forms reduce the effort needed to make independent choices across races. Such ballots are associated with higher rates of split-ticket voting, undermining the party coattails in down-ballot races. Our evidence indicates that in Salta the implementation of an electronic-based Australian ballot, in place of the traditional partisan paper ballot, is associated with a 4.6 percent increase in split-ticket voting.

After a voter splits the vote, some ballot forms increase the cost of reengaging in the election, whereas other forms – the electronic ballot adopted in Salta, for instance – keep the voter engaged with the process. As a result, the electronic device is linked to lower levels of voter roll-off, and heightened participation in down-ballot races. As a matter of fact, our analysis shows a 2.5 percent reduction in roll-off in province House elections in precincts using the electronic ballot, as compared to those using the partisan paper ballot. More generally, the effect of the ballot structure on voting behavior ultimately depends on the differences between ballots. Evidence from our study indicates that the Australian ballot administered via electronic devices in Salta, simultaneously increased split-ticket voting and reduced ballot roll-off.

Changes in ballots also reshape parties' incentives. The ballot reform in Salta affected the opportunities for small parties to increase their vote share by reducing the centrality of the gubernatorial candidates and allowing the party to strategically decide where to campaign. Campaigns in Argentina, as is typical in presidential democracies, are centered on the executive candidate, including governors in federal countries (Carlin and Singh 2015; Benton 2005). As split-ticket voting becomes more common, however, parties without a viable executive candidate at the top of the ticket may spend more time and resources campaigning around candidates in down-ballot races. Moreover, parties may spend campaign resources coaching voters to split their ballot – an established strategy among parties competing solely in down-ballot races.

Evidence from our work shows that the electronic device adopted in Salta created new electoral opportunities for smaller parties: up to 3 percent to 5 percent differences in vote share between gubernatorial and legislative candidates from the same party can be attributed to ballot structure alone. Under ballot structures that facilitate split-ticket voting, this strategy may become more common, and it might be pursued even against the will of party authorities with little tools to contain it.

Ballot design may influence the costs of competing across the entire district. Electioneering demands time and money. In Argentina – under the ballot and envelope system – individual parties are responsible for supplying their own ballots. Small parties often lack the money or human capital necessary to supply ballots to all polling stations across the district. Some ballots reduce (or even entirely remove) the cost of supplying and replenishing ballots in polling places. The electronic ballot adopted in Salta, for instance, transfers this responsibility to the electoral authority. With the centralization of ballot distribution, parties can count on ballot availability everywhere. Hence they are free to campaign beyond the borders of their electoral fiefdoms, leading to lower levels of geographical concentration of votes.

This change is most likely to influence the vote distribution of small parties. The vote concentration of small parties in Salta fell about 17 percent after the adoption of electronic voting. The magnitude of the effect might be larger in other cases. The change observed here was smaller than the one witnessed in Colombia after a similar reform (see Alles et al. 2021). The smaller magnitude observed here was possibly due to the relatively low concentration of party votes before the ballot reform in Salta.

There are also reasons to believe that ballots may have implications for party cohesion. In particular, the ease with which voters can split their ticket may create incentives for down-ballot candidates to campaign independently of their party, ultimately weakening the influence of party brands over elections. Alles, Pachón and Muñoz (2021) observed a personalization of campaign ads in Colombia, after a paper-based Australian ballot was adopted to replace partisan paper ballots. However, the extent to which the ballot form influences party cohesion is weighted by other factors. In fact, in contrast to the Colombian experience, in Argentina party leaders retained control over candidate's access to the ballot. These gatekeeping powers encourage candidates to display strong party loyalty (Jones et al. 2002), potentially reinforcing party cohesion in spite of candidates' incentives to develop personalized campaigns. And, recent research suggests that larger personalization of campaigns, even when voters are allowed to use preference voting within party lists, does not necessarily undercut the ideological cohesion of parties (Folke and Rickne 2020).

Finally, ballot structure influences the visibility of candidates competing in down-ballot races. Some ballot designs increase the saliency of personal attributes, boosting the electoral chances of candidates holding certain personal traits (Tchintian 2018). In this vein, two personal characteristics were examined in this Element: gender and experience. Our evidence indicates that the electronic devices used in Salta do substantially favor incumbents in local elections. Incumbent mayors, who were already natural front-runners, enjoyed an additional 6.2 percent advantage in districts using electronic voting as compared to incumbents competing in districts using paper ballots. Likewise, there is some (albeit weaker) evidence that women fare better when splitting the ballot is more difficult. Combined, the results indicate that ballot structure can affect the salience of personal vote-earning attributes in down-ballot races.

The implications of this finding, however, may not necessarily be welcomed. Incumbents often enjoy a large built-in advantage. We observe that some ballots strengthen the incumbency bonus by reinforcing the importance of personal attributes. These findings indicate that some ballot forms may inadvertently undermine the competitiveness of elections, with significant implications for accountability in down-ballot races. To the extent that incumbents enjoy a larger bonus, it may be even more difficult for opposition candidates to unseat incumbents and harder for voters to ultimately hold them accountable at the polls.

Refocusing the Electoral Connection

Electoral institutions structure representatives' decision-making in office and the policies implemented by the government (Barnes 2016; Carey and Shugart 1995; Crisp et al. 2004, 2021). Most research is focused on the implications of major electoral institutions, such as the use of proportional rules, district magnitudes, open lists, or the nature of party primaries. However, the devil is in the details. Revamping the ballot design affects party campaigns and election outcomes, and in doing so, reshapes what Mayhew (1974) called the electoral connection.

A ballot reform such as the one presented in this Element, if applied in an environment with large district magnitudes, may have important consequences for executive-legislative relations and the centrality of parties in the government. Larger split-ticket voting is associated with more legislative parties and a smaller probability of unified governments (Cox 1997; Shugart and Carey 1992), favoring a more diverse legislature. Although this situation may increase the probability of legislative gridlock (Shugart and Carey 1992), it is an opportunity to improve substantive representation. As parties are required to cultivate a broad legislative coalition to reach a policy outcome (Calvo 2014), increasing the number of views that are articulated in the policy-making process (Barnes 2016), they come one step closer to the ideal consensual democracy.

The ballot structure also has implications for the scope of policies, by reshaping the geographical bases of parties. Presidents face larger obstacles to implement programmatic policies when legislators rely on local, pork-oriented legislation, making their adoption much more costly (Weingast et al. 1981). When parties effectively compete in a limited number of places, their campaign efforts and policy platforms are more likely to concentrate on localized demands. Conversely, parties fighting for votes from across the entire district, most especially small forces that were typically more limited in their geographic scope, are compelled to broaden their policy platforms, trying to develop a more encompassing policy message.

Reforming Ballots across Argentina

Overall, the partisan consequences of Salta's ballot reform did not benefit the incumbent governor, Urtubey, who actively pushed for the implementation of electronic voting. An increase in split-ticket voting weakens executive coattails making the legislative elections more independent from the gubernatorial race, which in the end favors small parties. Moreover, the state provision of ballots helps opposition parties to penetrate the incumbent party's electoral fiefdoms, weakening the electoral influence of party networks on the ground. It is true that a strengthened incumbency advantage reinforces the reelection prospects of incumbent mayors, most of whom were allied with the governor, but that is not necessarily a direct benefit to the governor. Of course, none of the reform consequences hurt the governor's electoral prospects. Urtubey was a popular governor, who won back-to-back reelections by double-digit margins. However, none of the reform consequences directly benefitted him either.

This raises the question: why introduce a ballot reform in the first place? Distributive models of electoral reform argue that politicians – and particularly incumbent governments, given their influence over the legislative process – seek to secure their political position when passing a new set of rules (Calvo 2009). The ballot reform in Salta, nevertheless, does not fit that pattern: there is no evidence that the reform improved the incumbent party's electoral position. One conceivable answer is that elites lack the foresight needed to think through all the implications of a reform, and their choices are informed by limited knowledge of reform outcomes (Andrews and Jackman 2005), especially when they are reforming largely technical procedures. Though driven by instrumental considerations, reformers might not be exclusively motivated by gains in the inter-party competition, contrary to what distributive models assume. Instead, elites can also use reforms to strengthen their own position within the political party (Cox et al. 2019, Schröder and Manow 2020). In the case of Salta, for instance, the prospect of a national political career may have shaped the motivations of a young, ambitious governor.

A governor seeking a future presidential run may see an opportunity to raise his national profile by modernizing province-level voting procedures. National visibility is a benefit that can outweigh the costs of potentially losing a few legislative seats. Urtubey enjoyed a comfortable majority in both chambers in the provincial assembly, and given that all the Senate seats as well as a majority of the House seats were elected in small districts, those seats were shielded from larger fragmentation and weakened coattails. Instead, the ballot reform gave him considerable media coverage beyond the provincial boundaries. He even toured other provinces to promote the adoption of electronic voting. It granted him the opportunity to develop a public persona around democratic transparency.

Today, voters in all the national elections in Argentina, as well as in the vast majority of the provincial ones, still cast their votes with traditional paper ballots. It is widely recognized that the partisan paper ballots are not the most efficient form of voting. This has prompted frequent criticism from civil society and pressure on politicians to consider alternatives (Infobae, 10/07/2020; Mustapic et al. 2010).

Will the successful implementation of electronic voting in Salta spur more ballot reforms across Argentina? At the national level, the Macri Administration (2015–2019) included the replacement of the partisan paper ballots within a larger electoral reform package, but the bill did not pass Congress. Instead, the provinces have been a much more prolific laboratory of ballot innovation. Ten years after the initial adoption of electronic voting in Salta, three other provinces have used electronic voting to elect province-level authorities, while a few other jurisdictions have developed some electronic voting pilots in local elections. However, the international spread of electronic voting has slowed down since then, and the push for its adoption in Argentina has likewise lost traction.

The potential adoption of a paper-based Australian ballot has attracted the attention of reformers as well. At roughly the same time Salta adopted electronic voting, two other provinces adopted paper-based Australian ballots – all the province-level authorities in Córdoba and Santa Fe have been elected using them since then. But even this ballot faces substantial resistance from some parties. Consistent with our empirical results, research indicates that the adoption of an office-centered Australian ballot would weaken coattails (Engstrom and Kernell 2014; Calvo et al. 2009; Katz et al. 2011; Rusk 1970), allowing for smaller parties to gain ground in elections.

Resistance to modernizing election ballots presents a final piece of evidence that politicians indeed believe that voting procedures are consequential. That leaders are willing to settle for inefficient procedures, fearing that reforms could alter their vote share and ultimately cost them a seat at the table, is a reminder of the ever-present trade-offs that accompany preference aggregation and the challenges associated with designing the ideal ballot procedures. Our research does not indicate that one specific ballot form is strictly superior to another, but instead, it demonstrates why politicians, practitioners, and voters alike should be mindful of the ways ballot procedures permeate the entire political process. Voting procedures have real-world consequences, and the most important one is how they shape the connection between voters and their representatives.

References

Adrogué, Gerardo. 1995. El Nuevo Sistema Partidario Argentino. *La Nueva Matriz Política Argentina*, edited by Carlos Acuña. Buenos Aires: Nueva Visión, pp. 27–70.

Aguilar, Rosario, Saul Cunow, Scott Desposato, and Leonardo Sangali Barone. 2015. Ballot Structure, Candidate Race, and Vote Choice in Brazil. *Latin American Research Review* 50(3): 175–202.

Alles, Santiago, Mónica Pachón, and Manuela Muñoz. 2021. The Burden of Election Logistics: Election Ballots and the Territorial Influence of Party Machines in Colombia. *The Journal of Politics* 83(4): 1635–1651.

Alvarez, R. Michael, and Thad E. Hall. 2008. *Electronic Elections: The Perils and Promises of Digital Democracy*. Princeton, NJ: Princeton University Press.

Alvarez, R. Michael, Thad. E. Hall, and Morgan H. Llewellyn. 2008. Are Americans Confident Their Ballots Are Counted? *The Journal of Politics* 70(3): 754–766.

Alvarez, R. Michael, Gabriel Katz, Ricardo Llamosa, and Hugo Martínez. 2009. Assessing Voters' Attitudes towards Electronic Voting in Latin America: Evidence from Colombia's 2007 E-Voting Pilot. *E-Voting and Identity*, edited by Peter Y. A. Ryan and Berry Schoenmakers. Springer, Berlin, 75–91.

Alvarez, R. Michael, Gabriel Katz, and Julia Pomares. 2009. Evaluating New Voting Technologies in Latin America. Caltech/MIT Voting Technology Project: VTP Working Paper No. 93.

Alvarez, R. Michael, Gabriel Katz, and Julia Pomares. 2011. The Impact of New Technologies on Voter Confidence in Latin America: Evidence from E-Voting Experiments in Argentina and Colombia. *Journal of Information Technology and Politics* 8: 199–217.

Alvarez, R. Michael, Inés Levin, and Yimeng Li. 2018. Fraud, Convenience, and E-Voting: How Voting Experience Shapes Opinions about Voting Technology. *Journal of Information Technology & Politics* 15(2): 94–105.

Alvarez, R. Michael, Inés Levin, Julia Pomares, and Marcelo Leiras. 2013. Voting Made Safe and Easy: The Impact of E-Voting on Citizen Perceptions. *Political Science Research and Methods* 1(1): 117–137.

Andrews, Josephine T., and Robert W. Jackman. 2005. Strategic Fools: Electoral Rule Choice under Extreme Uncertainty. *Electoral Studies* 24(1): 65–84.

Ansolabehere, Stephen, James M. Snyder, Jr., and Charles Stewart, III. 2001. Candidate Positioning in US House Elections. *American Journal of Political Science* 45(1): 136–159.

Ansolabehere, Stephen, and Charles Stewart, III. 2005. Residual Votes Attributable to Technology. *The Journal of Politics* 67(2): 365–389.

Anzia, Sarah and Rachel Bernhard. 2022. Gender Stereotyping and the Electoral Success of Women Candidates: New Evidence from Local Elections in the United States. *British Journal of Political Science* 52(4): 1544–1563. https://doi.org/10.1017/S0007123421000570.

Atkeson, Lonna Rae, and Brian T. Hamel. 2020. Fit for the Job: Candidate Qualifications and Vote Choice in Low Information Elections. *Political Behavior* 42(1): 59–82.

Avelino, George, Ciro Biderman, and Glauco Peres da Silva. 2016. A Concentração Eleitoral no Brasil (1994–2014). *Dados: Revista de Ciências Sociais* 59(4): 1091–1125.

Banducci, Susan A., Jeffrey A. Karp, Michael Thrasher, and Colin Rallings. 2008. Ballot Photographs as Cues in Low-information Elections. *Political Psychology* 29(6): 903–917.

Barnes, Tiffany, 2016. *Gendering Legislative Behavior: Institutional Constraints and Collaboration*. New York: Cambridge University Press.

Barnes, Tiffany, and Emily Beaulieu. 2014. Gender Stereotypes and Corruption: How Candidates Affect Perceptions of Election Fraud. *Politics & Gender* 10(3): 365–391.

Barnes, Tiffany, Regina Branton, and Erin Cassese. 2017. A Reexamination of Women's Electoral Success in Open Seat Elections: The Conditioning Effect of Electoral Competition. *Journal of Women, Politics & Policy* 38(3): 298–317.

Barnes, Tiffany, and Gabriela Rangel. 2014. Election Law Reform in Chile: The Implementation of Automatic Registration and Voluntary Voting. *Election Law Journal* 13(4): 570–582.

Barnes, Tiffany, and Gabriela Rangel. 2018. Subnational Patterns of Participation: Compulsory Voting and the Conditional Impact of Institutional Design. *Political Research Quarterly* 71(4): 826–841.

Barnes, Tiffany, Carolina Tchintian, and Santiago Alles. 2017. Assessing Ballot Structure and Split-Ticket Voting: Evidence from a Quasi-Experiment. *The Journal of Politics* 79(2): 439–456.

Bauer, Nichole. 2020. *The Qualification Gap: Why Women Must Be Better than Men to Win Political Office*. New York: Cambridge University Press.

Beaulieu, Emily. 2014. From Voter ID to Party ID: How Political Parties affect Perceptions of Election Fraud in the US. *Electoral Studies* 35(9): 24–32.

Beaulieu, Emily. 2016. Electronic Voting and Perceptions of Election Fraud and Fairness. *Journal of Experimental Political Science* 3(1): 18–31.

Benton, Allyson L. 2005. Dissatisfied Democrats or Retrospective Voters? Economic Hardship, Political Institutions, and Voting Behavior in Latin America. *Comparative Political Studies* 38(4): 417–442.

Bernhard, Rachel, and Sean Freeder. 2020. The More You Know: Voter Heuristics and the Information Search. *Political Behavior* 42(2): 603–623.

Blombäck, Sofie, and Jenny de Fine Licht. 2017. Same Considerations, Different Decisions: Motivations for Split-Ticket Voting among Swedish Feminist Initiative Supporters. *Scandinavian Political Studies*, 40(1): 61–81.

Bochsler, Daniel. 2010. Measuring Party Nationalisation: A New Gini-Based Indicator that Corrects for the Number of Units. *Electoral Studies* 29(1): 155–168.

Boussalis, Constantine, Travis Coan, Mirya Holman, and Stefan Müller. 2021. Gender, Candidate Emotional Expression, and Voter Reactions during Televised Debates. *The American Political Science Review* 115(4): 1242–1257.

Bowler, Shaun, Todd Donovan, and Trudi Happ. 1992. Ballot Propositions and Information Costs: Direct Democracy and the Fatigued Voter. *The Western Political Quarterly* 45(2): 559–568.

Burden, Barry, and Gretchen Helmke. 2009. The Comparative Study of Split-Ticket Voting. *Electoral Studies* 28(1): 1–7.

Burden, Barry, and David Kimball. 2002. *Why Americans Split Their Tickets.* Ann Arbor, MI: University of Michigan Press.

Cain, Bruce, John Ferejohn, and Morris Fiorina. 1987. *The Personal Vote: Constituency Service and Electoral Independence.* Cambridge, MA: Harvard University Press.

Caltech/MIT Voting Technology Project. 2001. *Residual Votes Attributable to Technology: An Assessment of the Reliability of Existing Voting Equipment.* Version 2: March 30.

Calvo, Ernesto. 2009. The Competitive Road to Proportional Representation: Partisan Biases and Electoral Regime Change under Increasing Party Competition. *World Politics* 61(2): 254–295.

Calvo, Ernesto. 2014. *Legislator Success in Fragmented Congresses in Argentina: Plurality Cartels, Minority Presidents, and Lawmaking.* New York: Cambridge University Press.

Calvo, Ernesto, and Marcelo Escolar. 2005. *La Nueva Política de Partidos en la Argentina: Crisis Política, Realineamientos Partidarios y Reforma Electoral.* Buenos Aires: PENT-Prometeo.

Calvo, Ernesto, Marcelo Escolar, and Julia Pomares. 2009. Ballot Design and Split-Ticket Voting in Multiparty Systems: Experimental Evidence on Information Effects and Vote Choice. *Electoral Studies* 28(2): 218–231.

Calvo, Ernesto, and Marcelo Leiras. 2011. La forma de votar importa. El impacto de los nuevos instrumentos de votación sobre la conducta electoral en las provincias argentinas. Buenos Aires: CIPPEC-COPEC.

Calvo, Ernesto, and Juan Pablo Micozzi. 2005. The Governor's Backyard: A Seat-Vote Model of Electoral Reform for Subnational Multiparty Races. *The Journal of Politics* 67(4): 1050–1074.

Calvo, Ernesto, and María Victoria Murillo. 2004. Who Delivers? Partisan Clients in the Argentine Electoral Market. *American Journal of Political Science* 48(4): 742–757.

Calvo, Ernesto, and María Victoria Murillo. 2019. *Non-Policy Politics: Richer Voters, Poorer Voters, and the Diversification of Electoral Strategies.* New York: Cambridge University Press.

Calvo, Ernesto, and Jonathan Rodden. 2015. The Achilles Heel of Plurality Systems: Geography and Representation in Multiparty Democracies. *American Journal of Political Science* 59(4): 789–805.

Campbell, Angus, and Warren Miller. 1957. The Motivational Basis of Straight and Split-Ticket Voting. *The American Political Science Review* 51(2): 293–312.

Carey, John, and Matthew Søberg Shugart. 1995. Incentives to Cultivate a Personal Vote: A Rank Ordering of Electoral Formulas. *Electoral Studies* 14(4): 417–439.

Carlin, Ryan, and Shane Singh. 2015. Executive Power and Economic Accountability. *The Journal of Politics* 77(4): 1031–1044.

Carson, Jamie, and Jason Matthew Roberts. 2013. *Ambition, Competition, and Electoral Reform: The Politics of Congressional Elections across Time.* Ann Arbor, MI: University of Michigan Press.

Carty, Kenneth and Munroe Eagles. 1999. Do Local Campaigns Matter? Campaign Spending, the Local Canvass and Party Support in Canada. *Electoral Studies* 18(1): 69–87.

Casas, Agustin, Guillermo Diaz, and Christos Mavridis. 2020. How Influential Is Ballot Design in Elections? *Journal of Elections, Public Opinion and Parties.* https://doi.org/10.1080/17457289.2020.1844219.

Cox, Gary. 1997. *Making Votes Count: Strategic Coordination in the World's Electoral Systems.* Cambridge, MA: Cambridge University Press.

Cox, Gary, Jon Fiva, and Daniel Smith. 2019. Parties, Legislators, and the Origins of Proportional Representation. *Comparative Political Studies* 52 (1): 102–133.

Cribari-Neto, Francisco, and Achim Zeileis. 2010. Beta Regression in R. *Journal of Statistical Software* 34(2): 1–24.

Crisp, Brian, Maria Escobar-Lemmon, Bradford Jones, Mark Jones, and Michelle Taylor-Robinson. 2004. Vote-Seeking Incentives and Legislative Representation in Six Presidential Democracies. *The Journal of Politics* 66 (3): 823–846.

Crisp, Brian, Benjamin Schneider, Amy Catalinac, and Taishi Muraoka. 2021. Capturing Vote-Seeking Incentives and the Cultivation of a Personal and Party Vote. *Electoral Studies* 72. https://doi.org/10.1016/j.electstud.2021 .102369.

Darcy, Robert, and Anne Schneider. 1989. Confusing Ballots, Roll-off, and the Black Vote. *The Western Political Quarterly* 42(3): 347–364.

Desposato, Scott, and John Petrocik. 2003. The Variable Incumbency Advantage: New Voters, Redistricting, and the Personal Vote. *American Journal of Political Science* 47(1): 18–32.

Di Primio, Leandro. 2019. Implementación de tecnologías electrónicas al proceso de votación. *Instrumentos de Sufragio*. Observatorio de Reforma Electoral, no. 5. Buenos Aires: Dirección General Reforma Política y Electoral – GCBA.

Dodyk, Juan, and Juan Pablo Ruiz Nicolini. 2017. Enchufes, espejos y ijeras: efectos del diseño de las boletas sobre el comportamiento electoral. *Revista SAAP: Sociedad Argentina de Análisis Político* 11(2): 365–386.

Engstrom, Erik. 2012. The Rise and Decline of Turnout in Congressional Elections. *American Journal of Political Science* 56(2): 373–386.

Engstrom, Erik, and Samuel Kernell. 2014. *Party Ballots, Reform, and the Transformation of America's Electoral System*. New York: Cambridge University Press.

Engstrom, Erik, and Jason Roberts. 2020. *The Politics of Ballot Design: How States Shape American Democracy*. New York: Cambridge University Press.

Feierherd, Germán and Adrián Lucardi. 2022. When the Partisan Becomes Personal: Mayoral Incumbency Effects in Buenos Aires, 1983–2019. *Journal of Elections, Public Opinion and Parties*. https://doi.org/10.1080/ 17457289.2022.2081696.

Ferrari, Silvia, and Francisco Cribari-Neto. 2004. Beta Regression for Modelling Rates and Proportions. *Journal of Applied Statistics* 31(7): 799–815.

Folke, Olle, and Johanna Rickne. 2020. Who Wins Preference Votes? An Analysis of Party Loyalty, Ideology, and Accountability to Voters. *Journal of Theoretical Politics* 32(1): 11–35.

Fujiwara, Thomas. 2015. Voting Technology, Political Responsiveness, and Infant Health: Evidence from Brazil. *Econometrica* 83(2): 423–464.

Gamboa, Ricardo. 2011. Changing Electoral Rules: The Australian Ballot and Electoral Pacts in Chile (1958–1962). *Revista de Ciencia Política* 31(2): 159–186.

Garay, Candelaria, and Maria Marta Maroto. 2019. Local Health Care Provision as a Territorial Power-Building Strategy: Non-Aligned Mayors in Argentina. *Comparative Politics* 52(1): 105–134.

Garay, Candelaria, and Emilia Simison. 2022. When Mayors Deliver: Political Alignment and Well-being. *Studies in Comparative International Development* 57: 303–336. https://doi.org/10.1007/s12116-022-09357-w.

Gelman, Andrew, and Gary King. 1990. Estimating Incumbency Advantage without Bias. *American Journal of Political Science* 34(4): 1142–1164.

Gerber, Alan, and Donald Green. 2012. *Field Experiments: Design, Analysis, and Interpretation*. New York: Norton.

Gimpel, James, Frances Lee, and Joshua Kaminski. 2006. The Political Geography of Campaign Contributions in American Politics. *The Journal of Politics* 68(3): 626–639.

Gimpel, James, Frances Lee, and Shanna Pearson-Merkowitz. 2008. The Check Is in the Mail: Interdistrict Funding Flows in Congressional Elections. *American Journal of Political Science* 52(2): 373–394.

Gudgin, Graham, and Peter Taylor. 1976. The Myth of Non-Partisan Cartography: A Study of Electoral Biases in the English Boundary Commission's Redistribution for 1955–1970. *Urban Studies* 13(1): 13–25.

Hagopian, Frances, and Scott Mainwaring. eds. 2005. *The Third Wave of Democratization in Latin America: Advances and Setbacks*. New York: Cambridge University Press.

Hanmer, Michael J., Won Ho Park, Michael W. Traugott et al. 2010. Losing Fewer Votes: The Impact of Changing Voting Systems on Residual Votes. *Political Research Quarterly* 63(1): 129–142.

Harbers, Imke. 2017. Spatial Effects and Party Nationalization: The Geography of Partisan Support in Mexico. *Electoral Studies* 47: 55–66.

Hartlyn, Jonathan, and Arturo Valenzuela. 1995. Democracy in Latin America since 1930. *The Cambridge History of Latin America*, vol. 6. Edited by Leslie Bethell. Cambridge: Cambridge University Press, 97–162.

Heckelman, Jac. 2000. Revisiting the Relationship between Secret Ballots and Turnout: A New Test of Two Legal Institutional Theories. *American Politics Research* 28(2): 194–215.

Helmke, Gretchen. 2009. Ticket Splitting as Electoral Insurance: The Mexico 2000 Elections. *Electoral Studies* 28(1): 70–78.

Herrnson, Paul, Richard Niemi, Michael Hanmer et al. 2008. *Voting Technology: The Not-So-Simple Act of Casting a Ballot*. Washington, DC: Brookings Institution Press.

Ho, Daniel, and Kosuke Imai. 2008. Estimating Causal Effects of Ballot Order from a Randomized Natural Experiment: The California Alphabet Lottery, 1978–2002. *The Public Opinion Quarterly* 72(2): 216–240.

Ho, Daniel, Kosuke Imai, Gary King, and Elizabeth Stuart. 2007. Matching as Nonparametric Preprocessing for Reducing Model Dependence in Parametric Causal Inference. *Political Analysis* 15(3): 199–236.

Holman, Mirya, and Celeste Lay. 2021. Are You Picking Up What I Am Laying Down? Ideology in Low-Information Elections. *Urban Affairs Review* 57(2): 315–341.

Iacus, Stefano, Gary King, and Giuseppe Porro. 2012. Causal Inference without Balance Checking: Coarsened Exact Matching. *Political Analysis* 20(1): 1–24.

INDEC. 2010. *Censo Nacional de Población, Hogares y Viviendas 2010*. Buenos Aires: Instituto Nacional de Estadística y Censos.

Jones, Mark, Sebastián Saiegh, Pablo Spiller, and Mariano Tommasi. 2002. Amateur Legislators-Professional Politicians: The Consequences of Party-Centered Electoral Rules in a Federal System. *American Journal of Political Science* 46(3): 656–669.

Katz, Gabriel, Michael Alvarez, Ernesto Calvo, Marcelo Escolar, and Julia Pomares. 2011. Assessing the Impact of Alternative Voting Technologies on Multi-Party Elections: Design Features, Heuristic Processing and Voter Choice. *Political Behavior* 33(2): 247–270.

Katz, Jonathan N., and Brian R. Sala. 1996. Careerism, committee assignments, and the electoral connection. *The American Political Science Review* 90 (1): 21–33.

Kimball, David, and Martha Kropf. 2005. Ballot Design and Unrecorded Votes on Paper-Based Ballots. *Public Opinion Quarterly* 69(4): 508–529.

King, Gary, and Richard Nielsen. 2019. Why Propensity Scores Should Not Be Used for Matching. *Political Analysis* 27(4): 435–454.

Lamb, Matt, and Steven Perry. 2020. Knowing What You Don't Know: The Role of Information and Sophistication in Ballot Completion. *Social Science Quarterly* 101(3): 1132–1149.

Latner, Michael, and Anthony McGann. 2005. Geographical Representation under Proportional Representation: The Cases of Israel and the Netherlands. *Electoral Studies* 24(4): 709–734.

Mayhew, David. 1974. *Congress: The Electoral Connection*. New Haven, CT: Yale University Press.

Micozzi, Juan Pablo, and Adrián Lucardi. 2021. How Valuable Is a Legislative Seat? Incumbency Effects in the Argentine Chamber of Deputies. *Political Science Research and Methods* 9(2): 414–429.

Miller, Joanne M., and Jon A. Krosnick. 1998. The Impact of Candidate Name Order on Election Outcomes. *Public Opinion Quarterly* 62(3): 291–330.

Moehler, Devra, and Jeffrey Conroy-Krutz. 2016. Eyes on the Ballot: Priming Effects and Ethnic Voting in the Developing World. *Electoral Studies* 42: 99–113.

Morgan, Jana, and Melissa Buice. 2013. Latin American Attitudes toward Women in Politics: The Influence of Elite Cues, Female Advancement, and Individual Characteristics. *The American Political Science Review* 107(4): 644–662.

Moser, Robert, and Ethan Scheiner. 2009. Strategic Voting in Established and New Democracies: Ticket Splitting in Mixed-member Electoral Systems. *Electoral Studies* 28(1): 51–61.

Muraoka, Taishi. 2021. The Electoral Implications of Politically Irrelevant Cues under Demanding Electoral Systems. *Political Science Research and Methods* 9(2): 312–326.

Mustapic, Ana María, Gerardo Scherlis, and María Page. 2010. Boleta única. Agenda para avanzar hacia un modelo técnicamente sólido y políticamente viable. CIPPEC Working Paper No. 94.

Mustillo, Thomas, and John Polga-Hecimovich. 2020. Party, Candidate, and Voter Incentives under Free List Proportional Representation. *Journal of Theoretical Politics* 32(1): 143–167.

Nicolau, Jairo. 2012. *Eleições no Brasil: Do Império aos dias atuais*. Zahar.

Nicolau, Jairo. 2015. Impact of Electronic Voting Machines on Blank Votes and Null Votes in Brazilian Elections in 1998. *Brazilian Political Science Review* 9(3): 3–20.

Observatorio Político Electoral. 2021. Normativa comparada provincial. Buenos Aires: Ministerio del Interior. www.argentina.gob.ar/interior/observatorioelectoral/analisis/normativacomparada (accessed April 15, 2021).

Ortega Villodres, Carmen. 2008. Gender and Party Duopoly in a Small State: Ballot Position Effects Under the Single Transferable Vote in Malta, 1947–2008. *South European Society and Politics* 13(4): 435–456.

Pachón, Mónica, Royce Carroll, and Hernando Barragán. 2017. Ballot Design and Invalid Votes: Evidence from Colombia. *Electoral Studies* 48: 98–110.

Pachón, Mónica, and Matthew Søberg Shugart. 2010. Electoral Reform and the Mirror Image of Inter-party and Intra-party Competition: The Adoption of Party Lists in Colombia. *Electoral Studies* 29(4): 648–660.

Page, María, and Julieta Lenarduzzi. 2015. Cambios en la Forma de Votar: Experiencias y percepciones de las autoridades de mesa sobre el voto electrónico en las elecciones de Salta 2015. CIPPEC Working Paper No. 154.

Page, María, Josefina Mignone, and Julieta Lenarduzzi. 2016. Cambios en la forma de votar. 10 aprendizajes de la implementación del voto electrónico en la provincia de Salta. CIPPEC: Working Paper No. 147.

Patty, John, Constanza Schibber, Maggie Penn, and Brian Crisp. 2019. Valence, Elections, and Legislative Institutions. *American Journal of Political Science* 63(3): 563–576.

Peres da Silva, Glauco, and Andreza Davidian. 2013. Identification of Areas of Vote Concentration: Evidences from Brazil. *Brazilian Political Science Review* 7(2): 141–155.

Pomares, Julia, Marcelo Leiras, María Page, Carolina Tchintian, Anastasia Peralta Ramos. 2011. Cambios en la Forma de Votar: La experiencia del voto electrónico en Salta. CIPPEC Working Paper No. 94.

Pomares, Julia, Ines Levin, and Michael Alvarez. 2014. Do Voters and Poll Workers Differ in Their Attitudes toward E-Voting? Evidence from the First E-Election in Salta, Argentina. *Journal of Election Technology and Systems* 2 (2): 1–10.

Pomares, Julia, and Soledad Zárate. 2014. Cambios en la forma de votar: la primera elección provincial completa de un sistema electrónico de votación. Salta, 2013. CIPPEC Working Paper No. 130.

Potter, Joshua, and Santiago Olivella. 2015. Electoral Strategy in Geographic Space: Accounting for Spatial Proximity in District-level Party Competition. *Electoral Studies* 40: 76–86.

Remmer, Karen. 2008. The Politics of Institutional Change. Electoral Reform in Latin America, 1978–2002. *Party Politics* 14(1): 5–30.

Renwick, Alan. 2010. *The Politics of Electoral Reform: Changing the Rules of Democracy.* Cambridge: Cambridge University Press.

Reynolds, Andrew, and Marco Steenbergen. 2006. How the World Votes: The Political Consequences of Ballot Design, Innovation and Manipulation. *Electoral Studies* 25(3): 570–598.

Rich, Timothy. 2014. Split-Ticket Voting in South Korea's 2012 National Assembly Election. *Asian Politics & Policy* 6(3): 455–469.

Rodden, Jonathan. 2010. The Geographic Distribution of Political Preferences. *Annual Review of Political Science* 13(1): 312–340.

Rusk, Jerrold. 1970. The Effect of the Australian Ballot Reform on Split-Ticket Voting: 1876–1908. *The American Political Science Review* 64(4): 1220–1238.

Saxton, Gregory, and Tiffany Barnes. 2022. Sex and Ideology: Liberal and Conservative Responses to Scandal. *Journal of Elections, Public Opinion and Parties* 32(2): 396–407.

Schröder, Valentin, and Philip Manow. 2020. An Intra-party Account of Electoral System Choice. *Political Science Research and Methods* 8(2): 251–267.

Setzler, Mark. 2019. Adversity, Gender Stereotyping, and Appraisals of Female Political Leadership: Evidence from Latin America. *The Latin Americanist* 63(2): 189–219.

Shugart, Matthew Søberg, and John Carey. 1992. *Presidents and Assemblies: Constitutional Design and Electoral Dynamics.* Cambridge, MA: Cambridge University Press.

Sievert, Joel. 2020. The Impact of Electoral Rules and Reforms on Election Outcomes. *American Politics Research*, 48(6): 738–749.

Sinclair, Betsy, and Michael Alvarez. 2004. Who Overvotes, Who Undervotes, Using Punchcards? Evidence from Los Angeles Country. *Political Research Quarterly* 57(1): 15–25.

Söderlund, Peter, Åsa von Schoultz, and Achillefs Papageorgiou. 2021. Coping with Complexity: Ballot Position Effects in the Finnish Open-list Proportional Representation System. *Electoral Studies* 71. https://doi.org/10.1016/j.electstud.2021.102330.

Stewart, Charles. 2011. Voting Technologies. *Annual Review of Political Science* 14: 353–378.

Szwarcberg, Mariela. 2013. The Microfoundations of Political Clientelism: Lessons from the Argentine Case. *Latin American Research Review* 48(2): 32–54.

Tchintian, Carolina. 2018. Ballots, Vote Casting Procedures, and Electoral Outcomes. PhD Dissertation. Houston, TX: Department of Political Science, Rice University.

Teele, Dawn Langan, Joshua Kalla, and Frances Rosenbluth. 2018. The Ties that Double Bind: Social Roles and Women's Underrepresentation in Politics. *The American Political Science Review* 112(3): 525–541.

Tomz, Michael, and Robert Van Houweling. 2003. How does Voting Equipment Affect the Racial Gap in Voided Ballots? *American Journal of Political Science* 47(1): 46–60.

Tribunal Electoral de la Provincia de Salta. 2019. Manual de Capacitación para Autoridades de Mesa. Sistema de Boleta Única Electrónica. www.electoralsalta.gob.ar/informacion/2019/manual-de-capacitacion-2019.pdf (accessed April 15, 2021).

Trounstine, Jessica. 2011. Evidence of a Local Incumbency Advantage. *Legislative Studies Quarterly* 36(2): 255–280.

Tula, María Inés. 2005. *Voto electrónico: Entre votos y máquinas: Las nuevas tecnologías en los procesos electorales.* Buenos Aires: Ariel.

UNDP. 2017. *Informe Nacional sobre Desarrollo Humano 2017: Información para el Desarrollo Sostenible: Argentina y la Agenda 2030.* Buenos Aires: United Nations Development Programme.

Walker, Jack. 1966. Ballot Forms and Voter Fatigue: An Analysis of the Office Block and Party Column Ballots. *Midwest Journal of Political Science* 10(4): 448–463.

Wattenberg, Martin, Ian McAllister, and Anthony Salvanto. 2000. How Voting Is Like Taking an SAT Test: An Analysis of American Voter Rolloff. *American Politics Quarterly* 28(2): 234–250.

Weingast, Barry, Kenneth Shepsle, and Christopher Johnsen. 1981. The Political Economy of Benefits and Costs: A Neoclassical Approach to Distributive Politics. *Journal of Political Economy* 89(4): 642–664.

Zucco, Cesar, and Jairo Nicolau. 2016. Trading Old Errors for New Errors? The Impact of Electronic Voting Technology on Party Label Votes in Brazil. *Electoral Studies* 43:10–20.

Acknowledgments

We presented research from this project at a poster presentation about 10 years ago. The poster examined the effects of the ballot design on split-ticket voting. The main ideas presented in that poster were published in an article in *The Journal of Politics*. We continued working on other aspects of elections also shaped by voting procedures, presenting this research in conferences and workshops. Two years ago, we thought that putting all the empirical findings in a single piece was the best way to present a comprehensive perspective of the outcomes of an electoral reform.

We received immense help from multiple colleagues. Rick Wilson, Mark P. Jones, Robert Stein, Royce Carroll, Mirya Holman, Jesse Johnson, Mónica Pachón, Ernesto Calvo, Facundo G. Galvan, Jennifer Merolla, Jeffery Jenkins, and several anonymous reviewers provided very useful feedback in different stages of the research process. Teresa Ovejero, back then clerk of the Electoral Court of Salta and currently Chief Justice of the Supreme Court of Salta, shared detailed election data with us. Guibor Camargo and Jean Aroom provided outstanding help reconstructing the geography of electoral precincts in the Province of Salta, and linking them to census tracts. We thank all of them.

Previous version of this research has been presented at numerous venues: the Midwest Political Science Association Conference; the Comparative Politics Annual Conference in the Department of Political Science at Washington University; the Southern California Political Behavior Conference hosted at University of California at Riverside; the Sociedad Argentina de Análisis Político National Conference, hosted at the Universidad Nacional de Cuyo, Mendoza; the Empirical Study of Gender Research Network (EGEN) hosted at Vanderbilt University; the Evidence in Governance and Politics (EGAP) meeting hosted at Rice University; the Institutions in Context: Dictatorship and Democracy workshop, hosted at the University of Tampere, Finland; The Martin School at the University of Kentucky; the Department of Political Science at the University of Kentucky; the Department of Political Science at Tulane University, New Orleans; the Department of Political Science at Rice University; the Department of Political Science at the University of Virginia; the Department of Political Science at Texas Tech University; the Department of Political Science at Indiana University; the Department of Social Science at Universidad de San Andrés. We thank all the participants and discussants for their helpful comments and insights.

We would like to thank the editors of Cambridge Elements in Campaigns and Elections for guidance during the process of writing this Element. From the beginning, they believed that a thorough examination of a subnational electoral reform in Argentina had the potential of bringing general lessons about the effects of voting procedures. The project would not have come to fruition without their support.

A previous version of the vote-splitting analysis in Section 3 and the findings in Section 6 were published in a research article: Tiffany D. Barnes, Carolina Tchintian, and Santiago Alles, "Assessing Ballot Structure and Split Ticket Voting: Evidence from a Quasi-Experiment," *The Journal of Politics*, 2017, 79 (2): 439–456. Unless otherwise noted, all translations from Spanish to English are the author's own.

Replication materials for all the results and findings presented throughout this Element are available at the Harvard Dataverse, at: https://doi.org/ 10.7910/DVN/BSD7B4.

Cambridge Elements ☰

Campaigns and Elections

R. Michael Alvarez

California Institute of Technology

R. Michael Alvarez is Professor of Political and Computational Social Science at Caltech. His current research focuses on election administration and technology, campaigns and elections, and computational modeling.

Emily Beaulieu Bacchus

University of Kentucky

Emily Beaulieu Bacchus is Associate Professor of Political Science and Director of International Studies at the University of Kentucky. She is an expert in political institutions and contentious politics – focusing much of her work on perceptions of election fraud and electoral protests. Electoral Protest and Democracy in the Developing World was published by Cambridge University Press in 2014.

Charles Stewart III

Massachusetts Institute of Technology

Charles Stewart III is the Kenan Sahin Distinguished Professor of Political Science at MIT. His research and teaching focus on American politics, election administration, and legislative politics.

About the Series

Broadly focused, covering electoral campaigns and strategies, voting behavior, and electoral institutions, this Elements series offers the opportunity to publish work from new and emerging fields, especially those at the interface of technology, elections, and global electoral trends.

Cambridge Elements ☰

Campaigns and Elections

Printed in the United States
by Baker & Taylor Publisher Services